portland
cheap
eats

portland cheap eats

200 terrific bargain eateries

EDITED BY
CARRIE FLOYD

SASQUATCH BOOKS
SEATTLE

Printed in the United States of America
Distributed in Canada by Raincoast Books, Ltd.

First Edition.
03 02 01 00 99   5 4 3 2 1
ISSN: 1524-9239
ISBN: 1-57061-196-3

Cover photograph: Rick Dahms
Cover design: Karen Schober
Interior design: Kate Basart
Interior composition: Dan McComb

Special Sales Best Places® guidebooks are available at special discounts on bulk purchases for corporate, club, or organization sales promotions, premiums, and gifts. Special editions, including personalized covers, excerpts of existing guides, and corporate imprints, can be created in large quantities for specific needs. For more information, contact your local bookseller or Special Sales, Best Places Guidebooks, 615 Second Avenue, Suite 260, Seattle, Washington 98104, (800) 775-0817.

SASQUATCH BOOKS
615 Second Avenue
Seattle, Washington 98104
(206) 467-4300
books@SasquatchBooks.com
www.SasquatchBooks.com

contents

acknowledgments

Many thanks to the contributors to this book, who willingly took up fork and pen: Alicia Ahn, Santha Cassell, Meg DesCamp, Karen Guth, Jenn Louis, Eric Lutzker, Chris Lydgate, Maureen Mackey, Lee Medoff, Kelly Myers, and Anne T. Wilson. A big whopping thanks to Kim Carlson, who not only contributed a number of reviews, but also gave sage advice along the way. I also thank my family and friends, for their suggestions and willingness to dine where they might never have dined before (there is such a thing as "too cheap"), and for their tremendous support when my plate became too full.

Kudos again to Anne T. Wilson for accommodating a changing schedule and diligently fact-checking the manuscript. Thanks to copy editor Uma Kukathas, and proofreader Karen Parkin.

And, special thanks to my editor at Sasquatch, Novella Carpenter, who with her calm, encouraging demeanor could not have made my job more painless when the deadline for the manuscript and the due date for my second child coincided.

— Carrie Floyd

portland cheap eats and best places® guidebooks

Portland Cheap Eats is part of the Best Places® guidebook series, which means it's written by and for locals who enjoy getting out and tasting the food of the region. It's written for smart, hungry people of all ages—people who know it's not necessary to pay top dollar to revel in a four-star experience. When we're eating on the cheap, we look for a lot of different things: restaurants of good value serving tasty food, preferably independently owned and run by lively individuals, perhaps touched with local history, and sparked by fun and interesting decor. In sum, the restaurant has to be worth visiting again. Would we go back? Would we recommend it to a friend? These are the operative questions. Every place listed is not only inexpensive but also recommended.

Best Places® guidebooks, which have been published continuously since 1975, represent one of the most respected regional travel series in the country. Each guide is written completely independently: no advertisers, no sponsors, no favors. Our reviewers know their territory, work incognito, and seek out the very best a city or region has to offer. We provide tough, candid reports and describe the true strengths, foibles, and unique characteristics of each establishment listed.

Note: Readers are advised that the reviews in this edition are based on information available at press time and are subject to change. The editors welcome information conveyed by users of this book, as long as they have no financial connection with the establishment concerned. Report forms are provided at the end of the book, and feedback is also welcome via e-mail: books@SasquatchBooks.com.

what's cheap?

Portland Cheap Eats provides 200 honest recommendations for great, inexpensive restaurants in Portland and its neighborhoods—stretching north to Vancouver, Washington, south to Tualatin, west to Hillsboro, and east to Gresham.

Our price range for choosing these places was based on dinner for two for $30 or less (including tax, tip, and dessert—and sometimes even alcohol). Many cheap eats dinners fall in the $10–$20-for-two range; some spots are even less. Breakfast and lunch at the majority of the eateries in this book fall under $15 for two.

eats tips

Some budget eating tips to remember: Diners and cafes often feature daily or "blue plate" specials that usually include bread, salad, and dessert—all for one great, low price. At more upscale cafes and restaurants, pairing appetizers to make up a meal may be a better deal than an entree. Happy hours in Portland (mostly at places too cushy for this book) can be a great source of filling, free (or inexpensive) munchies. At establishments that offer wine, consider bringing your own bottle and paying a corkage fee, often a better deal than even the cheapest vintage on their lists.

meals/hours

While a lot of cheap eats serve all three squares, some focus on only one or two meals, like breakfast or breakfast and lunch. Some places have a specialty food or particular meal that's not to be missed. As such, we've made a point of telling you which days and meals you'll find a restaurant open. But call ahead for specific hours, as these often change or vary from day to day.

cashing out

Every cheap eat listed here accepts cash. Some take checks; some take only local checks. We've indicated what does which, but note that the usual ID may be required in either case. For those sporting plastic, we've listed which credit cards a place accepts: American Express (AE), Diner's Club (DC), Discover (DIS), Japanese credit card (JCB), MasterCard (MC), and Visa (V).

alcohol

For those who want to know, we tell you, using one of the following: full bar, beer and wine, beer only, wine only, no alcohol.

kids, pets, and other appendages

As a general rule, where the food is cheap, kids are welcome. Many of the cheap eats contained herein, however, are pubs and taverns and, thus, may require a patron to be 21 years old to enter. If you're considering one of these spots and want to take along Junior, call ahead. Fido is, of course, generally not welcome; but also note that some of the aforementioned pubs and taverns, or those places with sidewalk seating, are in fact dog-friendly. Call ahead, though, to be sure. Cats and pot-bellied pigs are frowned upon; a well-mannered parrot on your shoulder is a case-by-case situation.

reservations

Ha!

smoking

Nonsmoking establishments are, of course, very politically correct and Portland is a very politically correct city. But it's not California and, so, many of the diners, pubs, taverns, etc. listed here do allow smoking. If this is a problem for you, just be sure and call ahead to ask what the policy is. Likewise, if you smoke and don't want to be left puffing in the rain, call ahead.

disabilities

Many of the listings here are smaller cafes, older pubs, and hole-in-the-wall food stands. Not all of them are easily accessible to those with disabilities. At the end of the facts following each review, there is a wheelchair icon indicating spots that are wheelchair-accessible. If you have special needs, however, you may still want to call ahead.

indexes and eatery info

Reviews here are in alphabetical order. When an eatery has two locations, we list each one. For establishments with more than two branches, we list the original or most recommended branch only; but the location designation indicates where you can find other branches. Each restaurant is indexed in the back of this book by location and type of food served. With some clever cross-referencing, you can find that Thai spot on Belmont in a jiffy.

reader's report

Please feel free to use the report forms provided in the back of this book (or a copy of one) to let us know what you think. The usefulness of *Portland Cheap Eats* is dependent upon the hundreds who write to pat us on the back, share a new discovery, or tell us we screwed up.

200

terrific
bargain
eateries

ACAPULCO'S GOLD

2610 NW Vaughn St
☎ *(503) 220-0283*
Northwest

 ✗ *Mexican*

Just blocks from trendy NW 23rd Avenue, Acapulco's Gold rejects the attitude of its neighbors and creates one of its own. Resurrected after a fire in 1997, you'd hardly recognize the difference: the same Mexican kitsch adorns the wall, a staff as hip and alternative as ever keeps up the steady flow of chips and salsa, and the kitchen continues to send out large portions of Mexican-American classics. From enchiladas to burritos, tamales, tostadas, and quesadillas, the range is wide enough to please most appetites,  even of those who think they might prefer a hamburger. For vegetarians there are lots of choices, from the cheese and bean quesadilla with olives and onions to the soft-shell taco loaded up with rice, beans, cheese, tomatoes, and lettuce. Margaritas come in variety of flavors and, after a couple, the life-sized posters of Bill Clinton seem right at home with the pictures of Frida Khalo. *Lunch, dinner every day; MC, V; no checks; full bar.* ♿

ALAMEDA BREWHOUSE

4765 NE Fremont St
☎ *(503) 460-9025*
Alameda-Beaumont

✗ *Pub Grub*

While the last decade has brought lots of good beer to Portland via brewpubs, few of these spots have given us reason to get excited about the food. That's beginning to change, however, with the new wave of upscale brewpubs that devote as much attention to the setting and menu as the suds. Located in the heart of the Beaumont neighborhood, the family-friendly Alameda Brewhouse draws out the locals like ants to a picnic with its hand-crafted ales made distinct with ingredients like sage, juniper, and Willamette Valley fruit. Inside this lofty warehouse, folks perch on stools along the sinuous bar or crowd into one of the honey-colored slat-backed booths (which in the right light look like harvest wheat sheaves) to sup on above-average pub fare: superb poached chicken quesadillas with smoky ancho chile accents, perfectly cooked salmon gyros with a dilly tzatziki, a rich andouille and crayfish rotelle, or the rock Cornish game hen with wonderful pan gravy. For those wanting only to nibble, try the cajun calamari, lemon pepper chicken strips with the pesto-cilantro ranch dressing, or the spinach salad. Other dishes include thick fish and chips; huge slabs of baby back ribs; a generous burger with tomatoes, onions, and lettuce; whiskey-chipotle barbecue chicken; a noteworthy Reuben; and other classic sandwiches. If you are still hungry, try the home-baked pies or exquisite cheesecakes. If you're still thirsty, you can take home a 32-ounce carryout of beer. *Lunch, dinner every day; AE, MC, V; checks OK; full bar.* ♿

THE ALAMEDA CAFE
4641 NE Fremont St
☎ *(503) 284-5314*
Alameda-Beaumont   ✖ *Cafe*

What started out as a cozy neighborhood cafe frequented for break-fast has quickly earned the reputation as a great place for a meal any time of the day. Morning standards are augmented by the inventive specials like the bacon, egg, and cheddar sandwich on toasted sour-dough; a grilled pita pocket filled with eggs, feta, spinach, tomatoes and green peppers; and French toast fashioned from baguette slices dipped in cinnamon–sugared cornflakes. Lunch features anything from the excellent Alameda steak sandwich with feta, roasted peppers, and grilled eggplant to turkey pot pie, meat loaf, vegetarian foc-cacia, burgers, and chicken sandwiches. Cre-ative salads include Jamaican jerk chicken, Thai chicken over somen noodles, and caesar with rock shrimp and bacon. Dinner, with or without the kids, is a no-fuss affair made  pleasant by the easygoing ambiance, linen-covered tables, and exciting plates issuing from the kitchen. Tempting appetizers, such as grilled sausage with polenta and apples and the Chinatown Nachos—won-tons covered with melted pepper Jack, tomatoes, and scallions—give way to savory entrees and exciting pastas, like the one tossed with a sauce of sautéed chicken, artichoke hearts, tomatoes, spinach, and myzithra cheese. Check out the dessert chalkboard for seasonal pies and specials like strawberry shortcake or choose a standard such as crème caramel, chocolate cake with chocolate sour cream frosting, or an amazing peanut butter pie. *Breakfast, lunch, dinner Mon–Sat, breakfast and brunch Sun; AE, DC, MC, V; checks OK; beer and wine.*

ALBERTINA'S

424 NE 22nd Ave
☎ (503) 231-0216
Northeast, Close In ✗ *American*

This place should be honored for spreading good karma. With the exception of the head chef and kitchen manager, all staff in the former orphanage is volunteer, and revenues support the Albertina Kerr Center for the Treatment of Physically and Emotionally Disturbed Children. In addition to offering spiritual nourishment, the food is pretty tasty. The inexpensive three-course lunch, which changes weekly, is surprisingly inventive. You can start with a salad or soup, follow it with an entree such as Florentine Ham Roulade, Oriental Chicken in Spinach Nest, or chicken pot pie, then finish with dessert, maybe tangy lemon ice cream or a sumptuous cappuccino sundae. There are two seatings daily, at 11:30 am and 1pm, and reservations are recommended. *Lunch Mon–Fri; MC, V; checks OK; beer and wine.* ♿

ANNE HUGHES KITCHEN TABLE CAFE

400 SE 12th Ave
☎ (503) 230-6977
Southeast, Close In ✗ *American*

Some know Anne Hughes from her coffee room at Powell's Books; others might remember her from the poster she posed for sans clothes a few years back (for art's sake, OK?). And then there are those who've made her acquaintance at this cozy soup kitchen in southeast Portland. Lunch here means three soups a day—maybe Hungarian vegetable, chicken Thai coconut, and split pea—served with French bread, foccacia, or corn bread. Also offered at lunch are a couple different sandwich choices (along the lines of turkey, ham, or cheese) and salads. The cafe doubles as a neighborhood coffeehouse, making it a good place to stop in the morning for pastry and coffee, or to read the paper in the afternoon with a cappuccino and slice of homemade marionberry pie. *Lunch Mon–Fri; no credit cards; checks OK; beer and wine.*

AZTEC WILLIE & JOEY ROSE TAQUERIA

1501 NE Broadway
☎ *(503) 280-8900*
NE Broadway-Lloyd Center   ✗ *Mexican*

In one corner of this cavernous room, with its flying-saucer tables and high turquoise ceiling, is an attractive bar that serves up frosty margaritas by the pitcher. In the opposite corner is an inviting glass-walled playroom for the little ones. An unusual mix, but one that works to attract parents in search of mealtime distraction for both themselves and their children. Like its sister taquerias  Santa Fe (831 NW 23rd Avenue, 503/220-0406) and Mayas (1000 SW Morrison Street, 503/226-1946), the restaurant's strength lies in the variety of items available on the cafeteria-style menu. Diners move down a line, choosing between burritos, tacos, and enchiladas—half a dozen kinds of each, including such stars as the vividly flavored *chile verde* taco, the chicken mole enchilada, and the *chiles rellenos*. Cool the heat of your meal with fruity *aguas frescas*. *Lunch, dinner every day; AE, DIS, MC, V; no checks; full bar.*

BAI TONG

6141 SW Macadam Ave
☎ *(503) 452-4396*
SW Macadam Ave-Johns Landing   ✗ *Thai*

If you weren't looking for it, you might miss it. Located just south of Johns Landing on a stretch of SW Macadam Avenue devoted to the automobile, once you've discovered Bai Tong you'll find yourself returning by automatic pilot when the craving hits. Every meal begins with a complimentary soup that excites your taste buds for what's to come: fresh, crisp vegetables in salad rolls served with a hot and sour sauce; sweet *pad se ew* (wide rice noodles, broccoli, and egg), *massaman* curry (spicy beef curry with coconut milk, potatoes, and onion), spicy *pad khi-mao* (wide noodles with hot basil leaves, egg, and chile). Most entrees can be made with a choice of tofu, chicken, beef, or seafood, with the price adjusted accordingly. Lunch prices are slightly lower than dinner; both are very reasonable. Like the food, the atmosphere is clean and light, featuring high ceilings, ecru-colored walls, and abundant windows. *Lunch Mon—Fri, dinner every day; MC, V; no checks; beer and wine.* ♿

BANGKOK KITCHEN

2534 SE Belmont St
☎ *(503) 236-7349*
Belmont ✗ *Thai*

Portland's Thai restaurant market may have drawn some newer, more elaborate contenders, but crowds still stream here for the unadorned basics of Southeast Asian cooking: hot and sour soups, curries, tangy seafood salads, and noodles. The funky, informal atmosphere—with waiters in jeans and T-shirts and a no-frills decor—has attracted a faithful following of neighborhood locals and cross-river pilgrims who come for the family feeling and the famous whole crisp sea bass in chili sauce. Kids are more than welcome—the staff members wear their sense of humor like name tags. The Kitchen was recently sold, but don't fret—the new owners have promised to retain the name and great menu. *Lunch Tues–Fri, dinner Tues–Sat; no credit cards; checks OK; beer and wine.* ♿

BEATERVILLE CAFE

2201 N Killingsworth St
☎ *(503) 735-4652*
North Portland ✗ *Breakfast*

Kitsch comes to Killingsworth at the Beaterville Cafe, a sunny breakfast and lunch joint with an auto aesthetic. Chrome hubcaps and radiator gills add a certain sheen to the walls, while the Virgin Mary, ensconced in a bedpan, presides over this storefront cafe. This place is packed on Sundays—mostly neighborhood folks who look like they've vowed never to take a corporate job, or at least are trying to escape one. While funk blasts from the stereo, waiters—who've had far more caffeine than you ever will—serve up big American breakfasts all day long, and lunch after 11am. For something a little less ordinary, try the German pancake or curried tofu, then wash it down with a Reeds  ginger brew or fresh-squeezed ruby grapefruit juice. This is not a place to expect culinary wizardry, but for a good breakfast in a cozy space oozing with personality, you can't go wrong. Gossip with friends around a Formica table, or perch yourself at the beautiful wood counter and watch the orders come up; while you're there, tell the waiters to make the coffee stronger. Note that Beaterville is on North, not Northeast, Killingsworth. *Breakfast, lunch Tues–Sun; no credit cards; checks OK; no alcohol.* ♿

BELLA COOLA

6910 SE Milwaukie Ave
☎ *(503) 235-2233*
Westmoreland 🍴 *Tapas*

With the opening a few years back of Fiddleheads—a dressy, much-lauded restaurant in the heart of Westmoreland where indigenous dishes are given twenty-first century treatment—Chef Fernando Divina attracted the attention of diners from all over the city. At Bella Coola, the younger sibling of Fiddleheads, the food is also inspired by ingredients and preparations of the Western Hemisphere, from Brazil to Alaska, but is available in small dishes— almost all of which are priced under $5. You might have to twist your tongue to order the Xuxu Salad, but you'll be rewarded by a luscious sunburst in the mouth made with oranges and grated *chayote*. Oysters on the half-shell arrive iced with sangrita and taste as fresh as if they had just been plucked from the Pacific. There is a variety of hot tapas as well; the Yucatan-style pork tacos are already legendary. The ceilings in Bella Coola soar, and if you're expecting the foresty decor of Fiddleheads, there's an airiness and lightness to the postmodern space that might surprise you. *Lunch, dinner every day; AE, DIS, MC, V; no checks; full bar.*♿

BESAW'S

2301 NW Savier St
☎ *(503) 228-2619*
Northwest 🍴 *Bistro*

In the best tradition of the neighborhood cafe, Besaw's serves three squares a day in a bright, high-ceilinged dining room that beckons the neighbors—as well as others from well beyond the reaches of Nob Hill—to come back for repeat performances. The place has been here since the turn of the century, and it has aged beautifully; everything seems polished, from the mirror above the bar to the gracious service to the dinner menu that changes nightly. To dine inexpensively, how-ever, means going for breakfast or lunch. For morning fare you might try a hearty helping of Farmer's Hash with chunks of peppers and potatoes, or French toast. Lunch standouts include the meat loaf sandwich or the classic hamburger—especially when paired with a glass of Hefeweizen. *Breakfast, lunch Tues–Sun, dinner Tues–Sat; MC, V; checks OK; full bar.* &

BIG DAN'S WEST COAST BENTO

2346 NW Westover Rd
☎ *(503) 227-1779*
Northwest   ✕ *Bento*

Though bento seems to be a trend on its way out, Big Dan's remains a big favorite and the line still stretches out to the street. The core here is the yakitori bento, a Japanese box lunch, for $4. Open only for lunch, this enterprise offers skewers of barbecued beef, chicken, lamb, or shrimp served on brown or white rice, sauced with a simultaneously sweet and spicy yakitori concoction. They also have a vegetable curry served over rice, and a couple of side dishes; try the *humbao*, a steamed bun filled with barbecued pork. Don't ask for Diet Coke; beverages here are as authentic as the sauce: tropical fruit drinks and iced coffee only. There is no place to sit, so plan to take it out. *Lunch Mon–Fri; no credit cards; local checks only; no alcohol.*

BIMA BAR

1338 NW Hoyt St
☎ *(503) 241-3465*
Pearl District   ✕ *Caribbean*

The scene here is the thing—both architecturally and socially. Bima has one of Portland's most dramatic interiors: concrete warehouse walls towering up to a layered bare-wood ceiling, the room splashed by color and asymmetrical furniture. Nights the restaurant fills up with people who have actually reserved tables—special occasion-celebrators, business types, and sweethearts on dates—but the bar is lit up by the Pearl District art crowd, who sometimes even eat something. Among the tastiest dishes at the bar are the wood-grilled skewers: morsels of squid are marinated in a habanero pepper/garlic/sesame mixture, grilled over an open flame and served with a heap of garlic mashed potatoes, grits, or rice; there's also lamb, shrimp, or chicken to choose from. The list of "small plates" continues, with crabcakes, burgers, and fresh corn chips; most cost around $8. Add a cocktail—Bima is just that kind of place—and you might just squeak in under $30 for two. *Lunch, dinner Mon–Sat; AE, MC, V; local checks OK; full bar.* &

BOGART'S

921 SW Morrison St
☎ *(503) 224-3369*
Downtown   ✕ *Soup/Salad/Sandwich*

You'd think it would be more obvious, but it actually takes a moment to notice that the walls of this Portland classic are filled with Humphrey Bogart photos. Amidst all the Americana, sports memorabilia, and plastic promotional blowups, this quiet lunch joint on the third floor of the Galleria doubles as a Bogart theme park. Of course, the menu pays homage to Bogie's movies, from the massive Sidney Greenstreet and Lauren Bacall salads (huge platters of fresh greens

heaped with ham and turkey, and vegetables and cheese, respectively, gilded with bacon, blue cheese crumbles, and homemade dressings like mustard-tarragon) to the sandwiches, like the open-faced Casablanca (a broiled breast of chicken with ham and Swiss cheese) and The Big Sleep (hot pastrami, onions, and melted Swiss). Bread choices abound for sandwiches—they have rye, French rolls, English

muffins, sourdough, and whole wheat. Opt for the potato salad over the chips; made fresh every day, you'll have a hard time remembering one as good as this. Burgers and soup round out the menu, and for beverages you can choose between real iced tea and cold microbrews on tap. Baby Ruths and Hershey Bars are dessert. *Lunch, dinner every day; AE, DC, MC, V; checks OK; beer and wine.* &

BRAVO ITALIA

4110 NE Fremont St
☎ *(503) 282-2118*
Alameda-Beaumont   ✕ *Bistro*

On warm days, Bravo Italia's outside tables host neighborhood kids enjoying Italian sodas, homemade sorbets, and gelati that highlight the season's fruits. What many don't know, though, is that behind this ice cream parlor facade this small deli can also turn out great cooking—breakfast, lunch, and dinner. Mornings are busy on the weekends, when regulars stride straight back to the kitchen window to chat with the cook while waiting for their lattes and cinnamon rolls.

Try one of the perfectly cooked omelets or opt for the Spanish pota-toes—a huge mound of spuds topped with a poached egg, melted cheese, fresh spinach, and salsa. The lunch and dinner menus offer a small but convincing assortment of pasta dishes, salads, paninis, and deli sandwiches. At night, adults cruise the deli case stocked with wholesome takeout options such as lasagne, black bean enchilada casserole, the special ravioli of the day, or macaroni and cheese. An early sit-down dinner might be a hearty pasta dish like the melanzane pepperonata penne—a satisfying meld of sautéed zucchini, yellow squash, eggplant, garlic, onions, and capers, topped with a red pepper aioli and served with spinach greens—or the fortifying fettucine carbonara, loaded with Parma prosciutto. *Breakfast, lunch, dinner every day; MC, V; checks OK; beer and wine.*

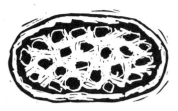

THE BRAZEN BEAN

2075 NW Glisan St
☎ *(503) 294-0636*
Northwest   ✕ *Lounge*

There's no place like the Bean when it comes to sipping a martini, watching a trail of a smoke, or meeting someone for a romantic inter-lude. The setting is pure nouveau Gothic—tables tucked into various nooks and crannies surrounded by deep, saturated colors, velvet, and lots of candles. Movie-set types of all ages comingle with Gen Xers to smoke cigars (there's a humidor on premise; ask your server if you care to see it), linger over a wide range of beverages—champagne, beer, cocktails, single malt Scotch, ports, coffee drinks, and tea—and nibble on the kinds of foods that go perfectly with drinks. Most of the menu consists of antipasto-type fare—like the assorted smoked meats and cheeses, or the artichoke pâté with foccacia—but includes a couple more substantial offerings such as chicken and cream cheese enchi-ladas and panini sandwiches. For dessert there's a chocolate silk pie, crème brûlée, and a messy but delectable chocolate fondue for two. *Dinner Mon–Sat; AE, MC, V; no checks; full bar.*

BREAD AND INK CAFE

3610 SE Hawthorne Blvd
☎ (503) 239-4756
Hawthorne ✗ Bistro

At this lofty, well-lit bistro in the heart of the Hawthorne neighbor-hood, longtime fans return again and again for what's become a fix. Maybe it's the ricotta-filled blintzes with sour cream and raspberry jam, the perfectly cooked hamburger served on an onion bun with homemade condiments, or a slice of *cassata* (Italian wedding cake) that lures the regulars; whatever it is, once you find your signature dish you'll be hard-pressed to order anything else. Though more ambitious (and pricey) dishes have found their way onto the dinner menu, it is still possible to dine well without spending a fortune if you stick with the salads, soups, black bean chili, and light dishes, like the sandwiches and burgers. That said, there are some who know only the breakfast menu here, a mish-mash of classics (pancakes, oatmeal, omelets) and Jewish deli favorites (bagels, bialy, chopped herring salad, lox). Floor to ceiling windows, comfy arm chairs, and amusing pen and ink drawings (check out the "State of Anxiety" piece in one of the bathrooms) only add to the charm of this corner cafe. *Breakfast, lunch Mon–Sat, dinner every day, brunch Sun; AE, DIS, MC, V; checks OK; beer and wine.* ♿

BRIDGEPORT ALE HOUSE

3632 SE Hawthorne Blvd
☎ (503) 233-6540
Hawthorne ✗ Pub Grub

Take away the boisterous element and what you have here is a fine place to eat. Spawned by BridgePort Brewing Company, the theme is beer, although that's easy to forget, given the upscale—especially for Hawthorne—menu and tony interior. Taupe green walls and cherry booths surround the cask-mounted open bar, the biggest draw for the twenty-something crowd. Everyone else grabs a table and dives into the menu: terrific pizzas (Italian sausage with roasted red peppers; grilled zucchini, mushroom, olive, tomato, and pesto) baked in the wood-fired oven in back; knife-and-fork sandwiches with exotic fillings of pan-fried oysters or grilled chicken and caramelized onions; and tasty salads. House specialties like penne with eggplant and tomato sauce or quesadillas with roasted vegetables or chicken pair well with the BridgePort beer on tap. To top it all off, try the marbled fudge brownie served warm with vanilla ice cream, or an old-fashioned root beer float. *Lunch, dinner every day; MC, V; checks OK; beer and wine.* &

BRIDGEPORT BREW PUB

1318 NW Marshall St
☎ *(503) 241-3612*
Pearl District ✗ *Pub Grub*

The folks hanging at BridgePort always look a little cleaner and more Ph.D.-ish than the rest of the world. Maybe it's because smoking is not allowed inside one of Portland's oldest brewpubs, and maybe drinking that great BridgePort brew—the India Pale Ale, for example—has a brain-enhancing effect. Who knows? The Pearl District locale near cobblestone streets and transient-filled loading docks is the essence of Rose City—especially on a night with a little haze. Friendly strangers share the long tables inside the cleaned-up warehouse, savoring the brew and sumptuous, freshly made pizza with loaded quality toppings like *chorizo*, artichokes, or feta on substantial, golden crusts made with—what else?!—beer. On summer afternoons, the loading dock is the place to meet, under the green ropes of hops hanging incongruously overhead. Upstairs is a party room that could accommodate the whole fraternity for pizza and beer, but again, things here seem to remain wholesome at all hours. *Lunch, dinner every day; MC, V; local checks OK; beer and wine.* &

BRIDGES

2716 NE Martin Luther King Jr. Blvd
☎ *(503) 288-4169*
Northeast, Close In ✗ *Soup/Salad/Sandwich*

Tabletop condiments nestle into empty microbrew six-pack cartons, sandwiches are served on flat baskets covered with gingham paper, and the atmosphere is cheery and funky at this urban breakfast and lunch haven. The "all-day-slacker" breakfast menu features eggs—poached or in omelets—as well as oatmeal, French toast, and black beans and rice. The lunch menu lists several "specialty sandwiches," all named after Portland bridges, such as the Broadway Hummus, Sellwood Caponata, and Hawthorne BLT. If you can't make up your mind—soup, salad, or sandwich?—try the combo; at $4.75 you can't go wrong. Despite the occasional flake factor, the eclectic crew tries hard to please, making Bridges a warm spot in a part of town that needs one. *Breakfast, lunch Mon, Wed–Fri; all-day brunch Sat–Sun; AE, MC, V; local checks only; beer and wine.* ♿

BUSTER'S TEXAS–STYLE BARBECUE

17883 SE McLoughlin Blvd, Milwaukie (and branches)
☎ *(503) 652-1076*
Milwaukie/Gresham/Tigard/Vancouver, WA and Vicinity ✕ *Barbecue*

Take a deep whiff. The wood-smoke ovens leave their mark on both the meat and the atmosphere. Brisket, links, chicken, beef, and pork ribs all pass through the cooker and come out estimably smoky and juicy. The barbecue sauces have a sweet brown-sugar base and come in three temps; the hottest demands a pint of beer to wash it down. Accompaniments are simple: fries, slaw, beans, and—for devils only—stuffed jalapeño peppers. There's an equal emphasis on barbecue essentials at the original Milwaukie location and the Gresham branch (503/667-4811). The Buster's in Tigard (503/452-8384) features a mesquite broiler, for those of faint disposition. *Lunch, dinner every day; AE, DIS, MC, V; no checks; beer and wine.* ♿

CADILLAC CAFE

914 NE Broadway
☎ *(503) 287-4750*
NE Broadway-Lloyd Center ✕ *Diner*

The bubble-gum pink stucco building exudes fun, and the interior decor is unmistakably diner-from-the-fifties. Especially popular on the weekends, when lines queue outside the door rain or shine, this place is known for its breakfasts. Fluffy buttermilk pancakes with blueberries, bananas, and hazelnuts and hot granola or oatmeal are surprisingly sublime. For savory there's the Tuscan omelet, a blend of sausage, roasted peppers, and Swiss, and the Picasso, with herbed chicken, mushrooms, and pesto cream cheese. The Eggs Mazatlan, two poached eggs atop a seasoned tortilla, tastes divine with the lemony guacamole and the not-to-be-missed crispy cheese potatoes covered with melted Jack, olives, green onions, red peppers, and salsa. Linger over a sumptuous specialty latte embellished with vanilla sprinkles or almond syrup, or a sparkling cider mimosa. Stay long enough, and you may consider lunch. The noon meal here means salads with inventive dressings like blueberry vinaigrette and cilantro ranch, and provocative soups like Zucchini-Basil-Tomato or mushroom Marsala, and numerous variations on the hamburger theme, all named after vintage Cadillacs. The Seville burger fuels up on caramelized onions, roasted peppers, and mushrooms, while the Coupe de Ville sports a rooftop of blue cheese and mustard-mayonnaise; any combination can be made with a Gardenburger substitution. Sandwiches range from deli classics to grilled cheese, sausage, chicken, and tuna. *Breakfast, lunch Tues–Sun; AE, MC, V; no checks; beer and wine.* &

CAFE LENA

2239 SE Hawthorne Blvd
☎ *(503) 238-7087*
Hawthorne   ✗ *Cafe*

This art-cluttered poetry den pays homage to poets both dead and alive. Tuesday night poetry readings draw an eclectic crowd with bohemian tendencies, while what looks like the entire surrounding neighborhood files through the door for breakfast on weekends. Do like everyone else does to endure the wait—bring a friend or the paper, as there never seems to be a rush to clear even empty tables. Once you get a seat, the general consensus is that it's yours for the rest of the day—or if you pen something worthwhile, maybe a lifetime. For breakfast there's Gertrude's Golden Toast (homemade challah French toast), Dante's Roma (two eggs scrambled with garlic, basil, parsley, marinated eggplant, and Parmesan, served with house spuds and a choice of toast, pastry, or scone), and good, strong coffee. Though known for its morning meal and late-night appeal, lunch and dinner are also worth noting for hearty sandwiches, fresh salads, and creative pastas. *Breakfast, lunch, dinner Tues–Sat, brunch only Sun; MC, V; checks OK; beer and wine.* &

CAFÉ MARX

2251 N Interstate Ave
☎ (503) 284-5629
North Portland

✗ Cafe

The minute you walk into Café Marx, you are aware that someone is obsessed with fishing. Not so, says owner Mark Lewis. The fish and fishing paraphernalia are about *fishiness*—"living outside of the box, being playful and surprising"—not fishing. Despite Mark's talk about relishing weirdness, his small cafe on Interstate Avenue is not weird at all, and neither is the menu: just straightforward, well-prepared, comforting food served in generous portions. A golden mountain of bread, made fresh on the premises, forms the backbone of the menu; toast, sandwiches, and burgers are all carved from this soft, hearty loaf. Breakfast offerings include biscuits and gravy, 12-grain French toast with peanut butter and maple syrup, and chicken-fried steak and eggs. For lunch there are burgers, chili with corn bread, sandwiches, and a daily special. And how about that fish that you might start to crave in such a fin-happy environment? If it wasn't for the token fish and chips on the menu, it would be the one that got away. *Breakfast, lunch Mon–Fri, brunch Sun; MC, V; checks OK; no alcohol.* ♿

CAFFE FRESCO

2387 NW Thurman St
☎ (503) 243-3247
Northwest

✗ Cafe

The breakfast potatoes, studded with seasonal vegetables and topped with provolone cheese, are about the only thing complicated at this neighborhood spot—hence their name, Complicated Potatoes. Everything else is refreshingly straightforward—especially the home-baked goods, which include a variety of scones, muffins, and coffee cakes (it's not uncommon to see eight different kinds of bundt cake in the case). There's also a 10-grain hot cereal laced with chopped hazelnuts and lots of brown sugar, or try the crisp waffles. Lunch features a soup of the day, a delicious house salad tossed with raspberry vinaigrette, and innovative—in a good way—sandwiches served on crusty Grand Central bread: smoked turkey with homemade salsa, vegan muffaletta with eggplant caponata, or chèvre and pesto with sun-dried tomatoes. Down the block from the granola-graced Food Front Co-op, Caffe Fresco has a natural, neighborly feel to it, but its quality can draw habitués of glitzier eateries. *Breakfast, lunch every day; no credit cards; local checks only; no alcohol.* &

CAMPBELL'S BARBEQUE

8701 SE Powell Blvd
☎ *(503) 777-9795*
SE Powell 🍴 *Barbecue*

People who come into this little house along Powell Boulevard and inhale deeply get more of a barbecue hit than some places provide in a rack of ribs. The dining area is quaint, the servers are cheerful and efficient, and side dishes—especially the potato salad and the corn bread—are inviting. But what packs the place is an exuberant vision of barbecue. Pork ribs, slathered with smoky brown-sugar sauce, are messy and satisfying. There are plenty of other options too, including smoked turkey, chicken, beef, and sausages. A space is available for parties, though some people claim any meal here is a party, and the party's never over until they've run out of peach cobbler. *Lunch, dinner Tues–Sat; AE, DIS, MC, V; no checks; no alcohol.* &

CASSIDY'S

1331 SW Washington St
☎ *(503) 223-0054*
Downtown 🍴 *Pub Grub*

With the greeting you get upon entering Cassidy's, you might well be at Cheers. A decent wine list and full bar accommodates many late-nighters and restaurant employees seeking fun after work, while an earlier crowd simply seeks satisfying food and friendly faces. The old-fashioned wooden bar is only a small step down from that at the White Eagle, and the menu is a step up. The dinner menu is pricey, so stick to the bar menu, which caters to many needs. From savory smoked seafood cheesecake to roasted Oregon mussels, there are several  options for a bit of reasonably priced but upscale dining. On the other hand, if plain and familiar is what you need, the grilled chicken club—a tender, marinated chicken breast with Swiss cheese and bacon—or a homemade version of a vegetarian burger, which features brown rice, couscous, oats, roasted vegetables, and sun-dried tomato pesto, might be in order. The fries are hand cut and crisp. There aren't too many other restaurants in town that serve such a selection until 2am. *Dinner every day; AE, DC, DIS, MC, V; no checks; full bar.* &

CASWELL

533 SE Grand Ave
☎ *(503) 232-6512*
Southeast, Close In *Bistro*

Depending on the night, Caswell feels like a neighborhood restaurant that just happens to have a bar, or a great bar that just happens to serve food that goes well with cocktails and beer. The best things on the menu are the smaller plates: bruschetta with goat cheese and sweet red peppers, grilled polenta with fresh mozzarella and marinara, cold tuna with olives and capers on bread. Pizza, pasta, and a handful of entrees such as gumbo and chicken curry round out the dinner menu, with the average plate ringing in at under $10. Lunch is mostly pasta and sandwiches, such as The Bank—grilled turkey and caramelized onions on homemade foccacia. What was once a cherished secret among southeast Portlanders is now a popular hangout replete with regulars from near and far. (Funny that the former occupant of the space, Starbucks, found the neighborhood not quite ready; now it appears they just weren't selling the right thing.) *Lunch Mon–Fri, dinner Mon–Sat; AE, MC, V; checks OK; full bar.* &

CHEZ JOSE EAST/CHEZ JOSE WEST

2220 NE Broadway/8502 SW Terwilliger Blvd
☎ *(503) 280-9888/(503) 244-0007*
NE Broadway-Lloyd Center/Burlingame *Southwestern*

The larger, flashier northeast outpost of this local southwestern favorite has a bar and a slightly bigger menu, but most dishes appear in both places—to general satisfaction. Chicken breast with a spicy peanut sauce, grilled shrimp with a chipotle honey dip, and the weird but truly addictive squash enchiladas span both sides of the Willamette, as do the specials on each blackboard. Sometimes a bowl of the rich black bean soup with a dollop of sour cream is all you need. The original Chez, with its iguana kitsch, faux-marble pillars, and

Lewis and Clark College hangers-on, is still highly popular, although its look is beginning to seem stuck in the '80s. Chez Jose East, on trendy NE Broadway, has a lot more seating, a booming bar, and garden tables outside when it's not raining. There's a kids menu, too, and at the eastside location kids eat for free every day from 5pm to 7pm. *Lunch Mon–Sat, dinner every day; MC, V; no checks; full bar.* &

CHEZ WHAT? CAFE
2203 NE Alberta St
☎ *(503) 281-1717*
Alberta St   ✕ *Bistro*

The clientele of this colorful bistro with its terracotta walls, blue batik curtains, and deep purple ceiling ranges from young and hip to thirty-somethings who look committed to art, community, and social justice. The vast, detailed menu offers an alternative take on American standards with a number of south-of-

the-border influences, reflecting the artistic, low-key gentrification of this working-class neighborhood. Service moves with a studied lack of concern, and meals take a while to arrive—but, so what? Customers never seem to be in a hurry here. Serving breakfast until midafternoon guarantees a relaxing time at Chez What? Cafe. Meat lovers can order scrambled eggs with *chorizo*, pepper bacon, spicy southwestern sausages, or Black Forest ham, while vegetarians opt for tofu, garlic, broccoli, spinach, zucchini, and various peppers. Cheddar, pepper Jack, and feta cheese are liberally applied to everything except the popular biscuits with sausage gravy. Lunch and dinner guests choose among overstuffed melts, massive burritos, huge burgers, and generous chicken sandwiches. The Laguna Tuna Melt arrives on thick sunflower sourdough bread with almond and cilantro nuances and mounded with avocado, tomatoes, and sprouts. The Narly Zydeco chicken sandwich is smothered in onions, mushrooms, peppers, jalapeños, pepper Jack, cheddar, garlic, sour cream, lettuce, tomato, and the provocative Chez Sauce—a combination of mustard, mayonnaise, ketchup, relish, salsa, tabasco, Worchestshire, and barbecue sauce that was surely dreamed up by a teenager. Homemade tortilla strips nestle alongside every order, or you can upgrade to crispy onion rings or gorgeous fries. Unusual desserts include Oreo or Snickers cheesecake, bourbon pecan pie, and Heath toffee crunch pie. *Breakfast, lunch, dinner Tues–Sat, breakfast, lunch Mon, brunch Sun; AE, DIS, MC, V; checks OK; beer and wine.* ♿

CHEZ'S LOUNGE AT CHEZ GRILL

2229 SE Hawthorne Blvd
☎ *(503) 239-4002*
Hawthorne   ✗ *Southwestern*

Chez's Lounge, the bar of Chez Grill, is a good place to sip fresh lime-juice margaritas, nibble away at chips and salsa, and fashion a meal from the bar menu. During happy hour (from 4pm to 6pm and 10pm to closing every night) most dishes ring in at $2.50 (except for · the hamburger, at $3.50) and follow Southwestern flavors: half quesadilla, soft taco, "Southwestern" caesar salad (with a spicy dressing and tortilla strip "croutons"), soup, rough-cut guacamole, or chili fries. The vegetable quesadilla, filled with mild cheese and earthy grilled vegetables, makes a tasty meal with one of the salads and a pint of Widmer Hefeweizen that flows on tap. After

work this place can hum, when an artsy crowd—as in graphic designer types in suits and heels—stop in to wind up or down. It's also a bit of a scene later at night when post-movie noshers come in to peruse an enticing list of mixed drinks and munchies against the upscale backdrop of gold walls with wood and black accents, cobalt blue lamps, and Southwestern-style art. *Dinner every day; MC, V; no checks; full bar.* ♿

CINDY'S HELVETIA CAFE

1212 NW Glisan St
☎ *(503) 221-0011*
Pearl District   ✗ *Diner*

Portland natives, locals, and conscientious tourists may remember it as the famed Shakers, where thousands of salt and pepper shakers lined the walls and those waiting for a table on the weekend waited outside, rain or shine. In 1998, Cindy McInnis, co-owner of the Hillsboro Helvetia Tavern, bought the place and named it after herself, not the decor. (Thank goodness; though the potholders and vintage plates add visual interest where the shakers once were, they would hardly inspire a very catchy name.) The menu—not unlike that of Shakers—offers simple, wholesome, no-frills diner food. Breakfast customers load up on griddlecakes, omelets, Scottish oatmeal, bangers, Cumberland Corned Beef Hash, or Meg's Vegetarian Hash. The lunch and dinner menu includes burgers (with a very popular ground turkey version), grilled sandwiches, soups, onion rings, and fries. The Cumberland Corned Beef, cooked on the premises and used in the best-selling morning hash, towers between two slices of rye bread slathered with homemade horseradish sauce, just one example of the lumberjack-sized portions (keep this in mind when you order the fries; a half-order easily feeds two). At press time there were rumors of ownership moving out of Cindy's hands. *Breakfast, lunch, dinner Tues–Sat, brunch Sun; no credit cards; checks OK; beer and wine.*

CLAY'S SMOKEHOUSE GRILL

2932 SE Division St
☎ *(503) 235-4755*
SE Division   ✗ *Barbecue*

There are two schools of barbecue: if it has sauce it's not real barbecue and if it doesn't have sauce it's not real barbecue. Clay's Smokehouse falls into the category of "more sauce is better," especially when it comes to the brisket sandwich—a delicious heap of hickory-smoked beef, onions, melted cheddar cheese, and the sweet and tangy Smokehouse barbecue sauce. All sandwiches and barbecue come with homefries drizzled with garlicky  sour cream and an unusual and tasty coleslaw enlivened with ginger and chile. The smoker on premise comes into contact with almost everything on the menu—the vegetables in the red bean and smoked vegetable chili, the salmon gracing the spinach salad, and the barbecued quarter-chicken served with hot links. There's not much to write home about the space itself, although the mismatched tables, green vinyl tablecloths, and faux-brick bar do lend a certain university pub feel to the place, with the friendly staff adding the warmth. *Lunch, dinner Tues–Sun; AE, DC, DIS, MC, V; checks OK; beer and wine.* ♿

COCINA DEL SOL

18770 SW Boones Ferry Road, Tualatin
☎ *(503) 691-2731*
Tualatin   ✗ *Inventive Ethnic*

In some ways, Cocina del Sol stands alone as a tropical island; there's probably not another place for miles around where you can start your meal with chips and salsa, move on to sizzling lemongrass beef strips eaten in a tortilla, and finish it all with flourless chocolate cake with Kahlua-laced whipped cream. The Tualatinos who flock to this happy, busy suburban hot spot don't seem to mind the incongruities one bit, and especially appreciate the lower-priced Mexican plates. A table on the screened porch upstairs helps you pretend you really have drifted off to a sunshiny place far from Portland—where a Black Forest drink concoction feels right at home with a panang curry and moist fish tacos. The children's menu—complete with buttered rice as an entree—will make even the youngest *campanero* feel welcome. *Lunch Tues–Sat, dinner Tues–Sun; AE, MC, V; local checks OK; full bar.* ♿

COLOSSO
1932 NE Broadway
☎ *(503) 288-3333*
NE Broadway-Lloyd Center   ✕ *Tapas*

Patrons at Colosso know that sharing an assortment of tapas, a bottle of sherry, and a stirring conversation with a table full of friends is a rich way to spend the evening—without spending an armload of cash.

In two low-lit, bronze-painted dining rooms, owner Julie Colosso and her staff cook up a dozen tapas and nearly half that many full dinners. Look for garlicky, piquant prawns in olive oil; wedges of grilled flatbread served with goat cheese and a basil pesto embellished with ground pumpkin seeds; and sautéed mushrooms with sherry and lemon thyme mounded on a thick slice of grilled bread. The menu changes twice yearly (with the two seasons in Portland, Colosso jokes), and there's always a long list of creative cocktails and nonalcoholic drinks made with such tantalizing ingredients as fresh grapefruit juice, coconut milk, or random pickled vegetables. By the looks of things, diners enjoy the drinks almost as much as the food. *Dinner every day; MC, V; no checks; full bar.* ♿

COMMON GROUNDS COFFEEHOUSE
4321 SE Hawthorne Blvd
☎ *(503) 236-4835*
Hawthorne   ✕ *Coffeehouse*

While it's easy to lament what Common Grounds used to be—namely, undiscovered—progress has not been wholly bad. Yes, they've packed too many tables in for the average paranoid writer, and sometimes there's a wait for a table (what next, reservations only?), but it is still one of the best coffeehouses in town. An excellent magazine rack, worn couches for lounging, windows for daydreaming, and delicious coffee—Torrefazione, served in a real mug—define the standards, while a panini grill and an expanded menu add to the welcome changes. Now instead of orbiting the pot of French press coffee that was going to be dinner, you can actually make a safe landing with one of the tasty grilled sandwiches and a bowl of soup. Other munchies include toasted Grand Central bolo rolls with butter and jam, wonderful homemade scones, bruschetta, and spinach salad. And, as with any coffeehouse worth its weight in arabica, there's nothing shy about the dessert case: ginger-banana cake with cream cheese frosting, chocolate mousse, lemon squares, and an assortment of cookies name only a handful of the offerings. *Breakfast, lunch, dinner every day; no credit cards; no checks; no alcohol.* &

CORNELIUS PASS ROADHOUSE AND BREWERY

4045 NW Cornelius Pass Road, Hillsboro
☎ *(503) 640-6174*
Hillsboro   ✕ *Pub Grub*

Amidst the rampant development along Highway 26 sits the old ImBrie Farmstead—better known as the McMenamin's Cornelius Pass Roadhouse, or, as regulars affectionately call it, CPR. Essentially a rural museum surrounded by high-tech sprawl and subdivisions, this anachronistic property boasts one of the few remaining octagonal barns, recently renovated and now open for receptions and private functions. The 1866 clapboard farmhouse houses the pub; its many rooms accommodate groups as large as a softball team as well as couples looking for intimate getaways. Pub fare—burgers and sandwiches—dominates the menu, but daring and delicious plates such as jambalaya and the irresistible Cajun fries are also worth pursuing. Microbrew fans appreciate the 12 taps of hand-crafted ale from the on-site brewery. Choose from a range of rich stouts, powerfully hopped pale ales, crisp golden ales, seasonal

specials, and the brewer's own creations. Outdoor seating in the extensive backyard and under ancient shade trees in front gives the roadhouse a festive beer garden atmosphere when the weather's warm, while the Little White Shed (the self-proclaimed "smallest bar in the world") makes a cozy, clubby gathering place for cigar and Scotch aficionados when there's a chill in the air. *Lunch, dinner every day; AE, DIS, MC, V; no checks; full bar.* ♿

COUNTER CULTURE

3000 NE Killingsworth St
☎ *(503) 249-3799*
Northeast, Close In   ✗ *Inventive Ethnic*

"Cuisine Nurturing Community" is the motto of this understated, light-filled bistro, which translates into incredibly reasonable prices for the paying clientele and a free plate of rice and beans for anyone homeless. In a working-class neighborhood where many businesses sport iron bars across their windows, Counter Culture has made a strong commitment to creating a community center for the people who live and work here. And though the profit margins may be slim for the ambitious owners, there's no sense of scrimping on either the decor or the flavor-packed menu. Breakfast features simple items such as bagels, muffins, and scones; standbys like quiche and granola; and such morning meal exotica as biscuit sandwiches, empanadas, and stuffed French toast, that come with sides of excellent garlic rosemary potatoes or fresh fruit. Lunches serve up gorgeous, freshly baked foccacia sandwiches topped with your choice of grilled marinated vegetables; zippy chicken with peach-chile chutney; or a combination of hummus, red onions, peppers, and lettuce. Daily specials have included a terrific lasagne that emphasizes the pasta, meat, and cheeses more than the sauce; teriyaki chicken bento; and meat loaf with garlic mashed potatoes, gravy, and a yummy biscuit. Tablecloths and waiters come out for dinner, and the menu changes weekly; past entrees have featured peppers stuffed with Mexican tabbouleh and served with an ancho chile sauce; chicken and dumplings; and beef Burgundy. Save room for dessert, including freshly baked pies, individual carrot cakes, or pôts de crème. Everything can be ordered to take home, too. With such good vibes and great food, it's a shame that this bistro can't be located within walking distance from everyone's home. *Breakfast, lunch every day, dinner Wed–Sun; AE, Mc, V; checks OK; beer and wine.* ♿

THE CUP AND SAUCER CAFE

3566 SE Hawthorne Blvd
☎ *(503) 236-6001*
Hawthorne   ✕ *Cafe*

Portland has many streets on which the Cup and Saucer might seem at home, but none quite so comfortably as Hawthorne Boulevard. Located smack-dab in the middle of one Hawthorne's busiest blocks, it's a great place to stop for a bite between record stores or after whiling away an entire morning at Powell's Books. Brightly lit, colorfully adorned, good-natured, maybe even a bit crunchy, this place gets through its massive weekend rushes with aplomb. A diverse crowd—tie-dyed, mop-dyed, glittering necklaces, khakis—comes here for the equally diverse menu. For those inclined, there's breakfast all day: your choice of eggs or tofu with the first sixteen choices of omelets, scrambles, huevos, breakfast sandwiches, and burritos. Other options include home-fried potatoes (with all kinds of things to gussy them up), French toast, pancakes, granola (with yogurt, skim, 2 percent, or soy milk), baked goodies, and side dishes along the lines of bacon, garden sausage, or brown rice. For lunch there are the usual suspects of sandwiches, daily specials, soups, salads, and a satisfying bacon-Swiss burger; though they don't hide the alfalfa sprouts here, neither do they shove them down your throat. Off-hours it's a great place to sit with a cup of coffee and thumb through Sappho. *Breakfast, lunch, dinner every day; no credit cards; checks OK; beer and wine.* ♿

CUP O' CHEER CAFE

808 SW 10th St
☎ *(503) 243-1461*
Downtown   ✕ *Cafe*

Is it the cheer they come for, or just the plain good food, when long lines of downtown office workers queue at lunch to place their orders at the counter? The deli case offers serious daily competition to the menu, with such offerings as spinach-mushroom quiche, foccacia with grilled veggies, squash enchiladas, and several salads. Top sellers on the small menu include smoked or roasted turkey breast sandwiches with combinations like citrus cream cheese, cranberry relish, and sprouts; Swiss cheese, avocado, and alfalfa sprouts; or bacon and cheddar. There are also two to four daily soups, generally inventive and wholesome, that come with signature Parmesan herb rolls. Early morning finds a substantial breakfast menu heavy on the eggs, potatoes, and bacon standards, with tofu available for vegetarian requests. Between meals folks wander over from the Central Library for a cup of tea or a latte, and baked sweets such as pear bread pudding. The nutritious food could be served less slap-dashedly, and how cheery the service is has a lot to do with whether or not the person behind the counter is or is not management. Some of the young counter help seem largely uninterested in the customers, though they hum nicely among themselves. *Breakfast, lunch Mon–Sat; no credit cards; checks OK; no alcohol.* &

CZABA'S BAR-B-QUE AND CATERING

5907 N Lombard St
☎ *(503) 240-0615*
St. Johns   *Barbecue*

When you see the giant black oil drums smoking out front, it's not too hard to guess what's on the menu. This ain't classic barbecue—classic barbecue doesn't have apricot and citrus elements—but it works, and people pile in for pork and beef ribs, hot links, and chicken, in adjustable degrees of heat. This place also does a mean catfish—cornmeal breaded and pan fried. Michael "Czaba" Brown, who somehow found barbecue inspiration while growing up in Portland, also puts effort and imagination into side dishes, like Southern succotash, collard greens, cabbage salad, and vivid garlic toast. Also worth noting are the special deals on certain nights: three ribs for five smackaroos on Wednesdays, all-you-can-eat ribs on Thursdays and Saturdays. *Lunch, dinner Tues–Sat; DIS, MC, V; no checks; no alcohol.*

DAN AND LOUIS' OYSTER BAR

208 SW Ankeny St
☎ *(503) 227-5906*
Old Town   *Seafood*

Tourists who visited Portland before the advent of the automobile came to this Old Town establishment for seafood—and out-of-towners are still coming. Among the place's charms are its value

($8.95 for the classic oyster fry, served alongside a hunk of sourdough and a haystack of iceberg lettuce sprinkled with tiny pink shrimp), and its coffee and pie (the marionberry is wonderful). Among its problems are efficient but unexciting preparations. The decor is family-friendly, with a lot to look at, from plates on the walls to maritime bric-a-brac everywhere, and you get the feeling that the Wachsmuth family has held their restaurant together through thick and thin for almost a century. You might encounter a setback or two—undercooked French fries, service that's friendly enough but absent for longer than you wish—but you may find yourself drawn to the predictability and charm of the place. Lots of regulars do. *Lunch, dinner every day; AE, DC, DIS, JCB, MC, V; local checks only; beer and wine.* &

DANTE'S RISTORANTE

111 E Main St, Battle Ground, WA
☎ *(360) 687-4373*
Vancouver, WA and Vicinity . ✗ *Italian*

From the outside, you may not even notice this hunkered-down gray building, but inside, the gregarious Caltagirone family serves up good-value Italian specialties like Spaghetti all'Amatriciana (pasta with a light garlic-pancetta sauce), Prawns Mediterranean, and predictable but generous full-meal-deal raviolis, manicottis, and cannellonis. Pizzas are popular with kids, and the revamped interior brings a touch of the trattoria to this small but growing town north of Vancouver, Washington. Desserts include a locally loved tiramisu. The food is hearty; the wine list is by the glass. *Dinner Mon—Sat; MC, V; checks OK; beer and wine.* &

DELTA CAFE

4607 SE Woodstock Blvd
☎ *(503) 771-3101*
Woodstock ✗ *Southern*

Just up the boulevard from Reed College is this hip hangout, decorated with ropes of beads hanging in the windows and Klimt reproductions on the walls, and serving steaming plates of Southern cooking on Formica-topped tables. The menu is pure Elvis, with some Cajun/Creole influence as well: fried chicken, blackened catfish, jambalaya, pork ribs, collard greens, mashed potatoes, corn bread, succotash, and apple-cheddar pie for dessert. No grits, but if it's comfort food you're after, you can get a substantial portion of mac-n-cheese for $3.50, with a hot biscuit alongside. If your thirst matches your appetite, wash it all down with a fresh-squeezed lemonade spiked with Jack Daniels—and still you'll find it difficult to spend $15 for dinner. *Lunch Sat–Sun, dinner every day; no credit cards; checks OK; full bar.* &

DINGO'S TACO BAR
4612 SE Hawthorne Blvd (and branch)
☎ *(503) 233-3996*
Hawthorne/Beaverton *Mexican*

Though the menus at both Dingo's are identical—lots of variations on things wrapped in tortillas, with a seafood bias and nothing over $7.95—the experience is not. The suburban Dingo's (11729 SW Beaverton-Hillsdale Hwy; 503/646-5998) is undoubtedly more refined—from its goldenrod and brick dining room with wooden-chrome chairs to its noteworthy service. The disheveled and rather dreary Hawthorne location is what it is: quick and cheap, but not a place to linger. That said, there are good things to be had at both, like the blackened shrimp burritos with cabbage and spicy sour cream and the chicken fajita tacos with corn, potatoes, green peppers, sour cream, and guacamole. An extra $1.90 to any a la carte selection upgrades it to a full meal, meaning you get chips, salsa, refried beans, and Spanish rice. For those inclined to eat on the run, you can fax in your order to guarantee faster service. *Lunch, dinner every day; DIS, MC, V; no checks; beer and wine.* &

DOGS DIG
212 NW Davis St
☎ *(503) 223-3362*
Northwest *Vegetarian*

The folks who work in the offices of the Portland Chamber of Commerce on NW Second Avenue have a well-kept secret that's just around the corner: it's this sliver of a vegetarian takeout spot, intriguingly named Dogs Dig. (If you need to know, ask super-friendly owner Sheila Gilronan the name's origin.) Bring an umbrella, because you might be standing out in the rain to get your lunch—which is worth the wait. Choose from a pair of delicious, wholesome homemade soups—

maybe potato and corn or curried lentil—or a substantial burrito. There are always mashed potatoes and rice (regulars often order soup on rice); there is always popcorn sprinkled with brewer's yeast; and there is always, always, always a plateful of tried-and-true chocolate chip cookies—made without eggs, butter, or any other animal products—that cost a mere 25 cents apiece. Dogs Digs' location makes it a good stop for a picnic; the Willamette River is just to the east, and a classical Chinese garden is slated to be built a block away in the other direction sometime in the near future. *Breakfast, lunch Mon–Fri; checks OK; no alcohol.*

DORIS' CAFE
325 NE Russell St
☎ *(503) 287-9249*
Northeast, Close In   ✗ *Southern*

Doris' serves full-scale soul food from oxtails to fried fish and greens—and its chicken wings could put Buffalo out of business. With its cool, attractive space of wood floors and high ceilings, Doris' has become a
meeting place in inner northeast Portland; other developments, including a jazz-and-coffee bar next door, seem to be rising around it. The barbecue smoker outside delivers a pile of rib tips with a smoky barbecue sauce that's more sweet than angry. The fried chicken's divine, and at lunchtime expect a run on the cornmeal-

dipped, deep-fried catfish and red snapper. Desserts vary, but if they're on the day's menu, the buttery pound cake and the mousselike sweet potato pie should not be missed. *Breakfast Sun, lunch, dinner every day; AE, DIS, MC, V; local checks only; full bar.* ♿

DOTS CAFE
2521 SE Clinton St
☎ *(503) 235-0203*
Clinton St   ✗ *Late Night*

It's a curious blend of idiosyncrasies that define Generation X: drinking Rainier pounders over microbrews, a cigarette in one hand and a Vegan Vavoom in the other, wearing expensive lipstick in a thrift store bric-a-brac decorated lounge. For many Xers, Dots is home—the perfect combination of food, friendliness, and freakiness—to return to night after night. Since it opened in 1991, for better or worse, not much has changed. Like the great pop songs that play on their stereo, each Dots experience feels familiar. The menu combines food for the meat lover (burgers, sandwiches) and vegetarian (burritos); all are tasty and hearty. The beer selection is not exhaustive but gives one a complete range of local flavors. Perhaps more diverse than it once was, the crowd includes longtime habitués who now have kids, and kids wearing knickers when Dots opened are now old enough to sit in groups, drink coffee, and eat large plates of cheddar fries. The moribund corner it opened up on is now a jumping hipster nexus. Your mother will giggle conspiratorially and say it's funky; your cousin who goes by Toad will nod gravely and say it's cool. Dots may not be as singular as it was when it opened, but now it may be, dare we say it, a classic. *Lunch, dinner every day; no credit cards; checks OK; beer and wine.* &

EL BURRITO LOCO

1942 N Portland Blvd (and branches)
☎ *(503) 735-9505*
North Portland/Gresham/Northeast, Beyond 39th   ✗ *Mexican*

This place is not for the faint of heart or the mildly hungry. The namesake creation is a fresh, floury tortilla bursting around a *chile relleno*, strips of tender beef, and refried beans. It's the kind of crazy concoction that you sometimes just gotta have *right now* and you can't find anywhere else. Tacos—loaded with chunks of pork, cilantro, tomatoes, and onion—are less filling, but they're so good and such a  bargain that you'll probably stuff yourself on a few anyway. Takeout is big business here (you're invited to call ahead); if you don't mind the divey decor, sit at one of the few tables and browse the spare copies of Latino or University of Portland newspapers. *Hasta luego*—we know you'll be back. *Lunch, dinner every day; no credit cards; no checks; no alcohol.*

EL PALENQUE

8324 SE 17th Ave
☎ *(503) 231-5140*
Sellwood   ✗ *Salvadoran*

The crisp-shirted, bow-tied waiters lend an air of affable formality to this Sellwood Salvadoran and Mexican restaurant, but at heart it's a chips-and-salsa (warm, crisp chips and not-quite-scorching house salsa) kind of place—truly addictive fare. The Mexican choices are *bueno*, but try the Salvadoran sampler for a real treat (not to mention a bargain, $14.70 for two or $21.40 for four): plump pork and *loroco pupusas*—corn tortillas stuffed with pork or *loroco* (an aromatic flower) and cheese, served with cabbage and hot sauce—plus tamales, fried bananas and cream, black beans, and rice. This is a substantial meal. Occasionally there's live guitar; sometimes the televisions are on. Almost always there's a brisk takeout business going on—another option when the addiction becomes unbearable. *Lunch, dinner every day ; MC, V; checks OK; beer and wine.* ♿

ELEPHANTS DELICATESSEN
13 NW 23rd Pl
☎ *(503) 224-3955*
Northwest ✗ *Deli*

For some northwest Portlanders, Elephants is more than a deli, it's a way of life—or at least a huge habit. We like Elephants when we don't want to go out, don't want to cook, can't face another bento box. It's a trusted means to eat delicious, gorgeous, homecooked food, and you don't have to cook it yourself. There are muffins, rolls, scones, and croissants to munch with coffee and fresh-squeezed juice for breakfast. The sandwiches at noon range from the classic (pastrami on rye) to the less-familiar-but-sublime (grilled Caprese: Roma tomatoes, basil, mozzarella, olive oil, and salt and pepper on Italian bread). There are hot entrees such as cannelloni marinara, and cold salads, including Greek, spinach, and curried chicken. The bakery makes some of the best breads in town (we love the Tuscan sourdough), and enough cakes, cookies, and pies to satisfy any sweet tooth around. What could be better? Of course, every

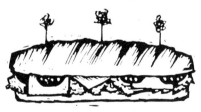

paradise has its price, and Elephants is no exception; but choose carefully and you'll get out of here without spending the entire week's grocery budget in one stop. *Breakfast, lunch, dinner every day; MC, V; local checks OK; beer and wine.*

THE EMPIRE ROOM

4620 SE Hawthorne Blvd
☎ (503) 231-9225
Hawthorne   ✗ Lounge

Though some might claim that all style and no substance is only interesting when it comes to costume jewelry and meringue desserts, others
will argue that there is substance in style. Either way, the Empire Room

is a stylish place to stall, to linger, to go after
you've been someplace else but you're not quite
ready to go home. Soft lights, small tables, a very
stylish waitstaff clad in black and platform heels,
and jazzy music provide the ambiance of a
French salon. This is not a place to dine, but to
nibble; the menu features more drinks—sherry,
port, mircobrews, espresso drinks, and wine,
both by the glass and bottle—than dishes.

Though much of the food lacks substance and comes off as merely
passable, it serves its purpose as a conduit for softening the blows of
wine on an empty stomach and breaking up the monotony of lifting a
glass to your lips and gazing across the table at your one and only-o.
And truly, the best things on the menu are those things that accompany either wine or coffee: the cheese and fruit plate, a sun-dried
tomato and smoked mozzarella spread served with bread, a bowl of
olives or pistachios, and rich chocolate desserts. *Evenings Tues–Sat;
AE, DIS, MC, V; local checks OK; beer, wine, and select liquor.* ♿

ENSENADA'S

3962 NE Martin Luther King Jr. Blvd
☎ (503) 249-7378
Northeast, Close In   ✗ Mexican

What looks like a blue cardboard box that will surely blow over with a
small gust of wind is actually the home of one of Portland's better
taquerias. Carlos Medrano, as upbeat as the Latino music that plays
over the speakers, presides over the restaurant, living out the motto "If
you have the time, we'll be glad to serve you." Everything here costs
less than $5, from the *tostada de jaiva* (with fresh crab) to the ceviche or
fried snapper tacos, truly vegetarian (vegetable oil, not lard) tamales,
and gigantic burritos filled with beef, pork, chicken, or beans and augmented with rice, cilantro, tomatoes, lettuce, onions, and cheese.
Breakfast is served all day, so you don't have to postpone a craving for
huevos rancheros or a breakfast burrito until you hear the rooster

crow. Trinkets, maps, posters, and postcards cover the walls, adding interest to the decor but not necessarily transporting you to the coastal namesake, Ensenada. *Breakfast, lunch, dinner every day; no credit cards; no checks; no alcohol.*

EPICURE
407 NW 17th St
☎ *(503) 916-1676*
Northwest   ✗ *Soup/Salad/Sandwich*

Traditionally, the word *epicure* has been used to describe a person knowledgeable about food and wine. Thanks to Debrah and Joe Vanchura, the husband and wife team who launched Epicure in 1997, the word may soon come to mean "as you wish" or "in lieu of the fast food drive-thru window." Ravenous lunch-hour diners choose from a fantastic menu of creative sandwiches, salads, and soups, to consume at one of the few tables, while the after-work crowd stops in to purchase takehome dinner entrees for the entire family. Combining fresh ingredients with a healthy bias results in dishes like the best-selling Mom's Old-Fashioned Meatloaf, a revamped recipe from Debrah's mother that uses low-fat egg substitute and extra-lean ground beef in place of traditional, high-fat ingredients. Other terrific takeout entrees include Italian chicken sausage lasagne, chicken relleno casserole, chicken pot pie, macaroni and cheese, and vegetarian paella; all are packaged in oven-, microwave-, and freezer-safe containers with reheating instructions. Also, the folks at Epicure will gladly prepare a family-sized casserole; customers can even bring in their own dish to be filled with the finished product. Special dietary requests, party-sized casseroles, delivery, and overnight shipping? As you wish. *Lunch, dinner Mon–Fri; MC, V; checks OK; retail wine only.* ♿

ESCAPE FROM NEW YORK PIZZA
622 NW 23rd Ave
☎ *(503) 227-5423*
Northwest   ✗ *Pizza*

On NW 23rd Avenue, down the street from the dog biscuit bakery and amidst the many espresso shops, hopelessly haute houseware shops, and multitude of restaurants that serve almost anything your heart desires, sits this dependable storefront that offers one thing and one

thing only: the classic
Gotham pie—thin crust,
spicy tomato sauce, and
a massive layer of cheese.
EFNYP pizza is the closest
thing to New York ferry
pizza—as in greasy and

floppy—that you'll find in this metropolis. There are but a few choices
of toppings available on pizzas by the slice—cheese, pepperoni, and a
daily special like olive and mushroom. There's a laid-back postcard-
and-graffiti-style ambiance that has so far admirably resisted gentrification. The servers are sometimes nice, never effusive, and it's a
contest between them and the patrons when it comes to numbers of
tattoos and piercings. *Lunch, dinner every day; no credit cards; local
checks only; beer and wine.* &

FAT CITY CAFE

7820 SW Capitol Hwy
☎ *(503) 245-5457*
Multnomah   ✗ *Diner*

One look at the generous scoop of butter sitting atop the enormous
pancakes and you know why this place wasn't called Skinny City. One
taste and you probably won't mind. Nothing is subtle, but that's fine
with the regulars, who fill up this storefront in Multnomah just as
they've been doing for years. Apparently it's fine, too, with the legions
of newcomers who keep rolling into the village. The ham comes in
slabs, the omelets could feed a family of four, the gooey cinnamon
rolls are housemade, and the coffee is, well, hot. Lunchtime means
basics like burgers and fries, patty melts, Reuben sandwiches, and—
when the machine's not on the fritz—milk shakes worthy of the old-
time soda counter. *Breakfast, lunch every day; MC, V; checks OK; no
alcohol.*

FELLINI

121 NW 6th Ave
☎ *(503) 243-2120*
Chinatown   ✗ *Inventive Ethnic*

Next door to Satyricon—famous for its long tenure as Portland's
alterna-music headquarters—sits this hip lunch, dinner, and late-night
eatery, where the food is better than you might expect from a place
with so much attitude. The menu offers straightforward dishes from

around the world—Greece, Mexico, Thailand, Italy—served in ample portions. You might start with an appetizer of hummus, tzatziki, olives, roasted peppers, and warm pita—and not want to go any further. But if you do, try the Bangkok Ho, a mound of crunchy vegetables in peanut sauce on brown rice, or the Zapatistas, a fire-roasted enchilada plump with vegetables, cheddar cheese, and chili sauce. Gyros and burgers round out the global offerings. Fellini's food is good for you, even if the secondhand smoke, black-light paintings, and outdoor tables on sketchy NW Sixth Avenue are not. *Lunch Mon—Fri, dinner every day; MC, V; no checks; full bar.* &

FLYING PIE PIZZERIA

7804 SE Stark St
☎ *(503) 254-2016*
Southeast, Beyond 39th   ✕ *Pizza*

The eponymous airborne pie must be an O'Hare–LaGuardia shuttle, because this place makes its explicit task the equal representation of the styles of the two great pizza cities. The crust comes in four gradations, from a thick, true Chicago (or perhaps Sicilian in the parlance of the West) to an extra-thin New York style. As with many things, the truth may lie somewhere in between—but probably on the thinner side. The ingredients are fresh (a choice of 31 toppings), the conception good (you won't find a pizza with chêvre, walnuts, or hearts of palm on the specials board here), and the atmosphere just as sturdy and

inviting as John's of Bleecker Street. For heavyweights there's a 12-pound 18-inch combo with 9 toppings; lighter appetites can graze on the salad bar stocked with classics like crinkle-cut beets and bacon bits. Located in a gritty and undervalued commercial district along Stark

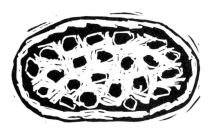

Street on the back side of Mount Tabor, this is a great place to take kids; a cacophonic video game room entertains the tykes while waiting out the interminable quarter of an hour it takes a pie to cook. *Lunch, dinner every day; DIS, MC, V; no checks; beer and wine.* &

FONG CHONG

301 NW 4th Ave
☎ *(503) 220-0235*
Chinatown ✕ Chinese

Just because Fong Chong has been a Portland dim sum pet for a long time, don't think the offerings are just the same old chicken feet. You might find something surprising, like shallot dumplings, alongside the

vibrant *humbao* and savory sticky rice in a lotus leaf. This is where Portland's dim sum devotees put the cart before each course. The much larger House of Louie, under the same ownership, is across the street. But whether it's because of the Chinese grocery next door, or because the place is crowded and loud, or

because watching the carts maneuver through the tables is like watching the Super Mario Brothers, we like Fong Chong better. It's fun, inexpensive, and impressively tasty. At night, Fong Chong is transformed into a quiet Cantonese eatery, with average preparations and a few surprises. *Lunch, dinner every day; MC, V; no checks; beer and wine.* ♿

FOOTHILL BROILER

33 NW 23rd Pl
☎ *(503) 223-0287*
Northwest ✕ American

Come in at noon and you'll find yourself waiting in line—possibly longer than you might have expected—with socialites, construction workers, and realtors talking deals. This is a step-up-from-a-cafeteria kind of place, where you can have a hamburger and a cupcake or a bowl of spaghetti and a malted milk shake. Burger patties come in three sizes—none will put you out more than $4.50—with good French fries or baked beans alongside. The cooks will even grill a tuna sandwich if that's the way you like it. The cafeteria line takes you past stalwarts like Jell-O with fruit and cottage cheese en route to some fine layer cakes, cheesecakes, and pies. For cheap snacks there are hardboiled eggs for 75 cents a piece, or asparagus for 20 cents a spear. Tile work, framed prints, and unexpected skylights in the back raise the interior from merely cafeterian to almost stylish. *Breakfast, lunch Mon–Sat, dinner Mon–Sat; no credit cards; checks OK; no alcohol.* ♿

FORMOSA HARBOR

915 SW 2nd Ave
☎ *(503) 228-4144*
Downtown   ✕ *Chinese*

At lunch, this skillful, reasonably priced Chinese restaurant downtown is jammed; at dinner, finding a table is no problem. But at both meals, the flavors are vivid and clean—from General Tso's chicken to brimming bowls of soup or noodles. Try to make it here when asparagus is in season: Formosa Harbor stir-fries it quickly with a choice of meats, and produces something that tastes like spring on a chopstick. The under-$5 lunch specials, from twice-cooked pork to shrimp with cashews, are highly satisfying. Weekend nights there's activity around the enormous two-story bar, but the more interesting events are happening in the kitchen. *Lunch Mon–Fri, dinner Mon–Sat; AE, DIS, MC, V; no checks; full bar.* ♿

FUJIN

3549 SE Hawthorne Blvd
☎ *(503) 231-3753*
Hawthorne   ✕ *Chinese*

While many Chinese restaurants rest on their laurels serving the same old chop suey and chow mein of yore, this one-room Hawthorne neighborhood favorite still ignites its culinary spark. A number of the signature dishes—heavenly crispy eggplant with seductive and creamy contrasts, plump and briny black bean–dabbed oysters, and beef or chicken packed with bitter-tangy orange rind and surprising zaps of heat—lift this spot up and over the competition. Execution is consistent, and service, while a bit brusque when it's busy, is lightning fast. For some the routine is this: order dinner to go, hop  next door for a video, and 10 minutes later you're on your way home with a contented, full belly in your future. *Lunch, dinner Mon–Sat; MC, V; no checks; beer and wine.* ♿

FULLER'S COFFEE SHOP

136 NW 9th Ave
☎ (503) 222-5608
Pearl District   ✗ Diner

Fuller's existed long before what has come to be known as the Pearl
District was ever born. This legendary stool-at-the-counter 1940s
coffee shop has built its reputation on standard diner fare and friendly
prices. From a bowl of oatmeal to piggies in a blanket (sausages
wrapped in a light and fluffy pancake), and your basic plate of ham
and eggs, there are no surprises here. No granola, yogurt, or frittatas,
either. Lunch at the counter means a French dip, club sandwich, hamburger, or fish and chips, with a thick milk shake, banana split, or a
slice of homemade berry pie to follow. Home of the bottomless cup of
coffee, they wouldn't even think of charging you for a refill here.
Breakfast, lunch Mon–Sat; no credit cards; checks OK; no alcohol.

FUSION

4100 SE Division St
☎ (503) 233-6950
SE Division   ✗ Inventive Ethnic

On the bottom of one of the menus reads, "Confusion says: You never
have enough stuff. . . let us help you with your retail therapy"—a perfect motto for a restaurant that doubles as a secondhand shop. Up
front you'll find a beautiful oak bar (a remnant from the '40s when the
same space housed a pharmacy and soda fountain) surrounded by
Formica tables (not for sale),
while the back sports sundry furni-
ture, dishes, and vintage col-
lectibles (for sale). Amidst this
funky setting, direct your attention
to the menu, which is anything
but secondhand or second-rate.
For both lunch and dinner there are an assortment of starters and
updated sandwich classics—like the ham and Swiss with mango
chutney—as well as salads and "light meals." The light meals average
about $7.50 and include such possibilities as the Fusion Burger, red
curry mussels, or a mesquite grilled half-chicken served with a black
bean–corn salsa. Vintage desserts—maybe a fudgy brownie or ginger-
pear bread pudding—complete the experience. *Brunch Sun, lunch,
dinner Tues–Sat; MC, V; checks OK; wine and beer.* ♿

GARBONZOS

922 NW 21st Ave (and branches)
☎ (503) 227-4196
Northwest/Hawthorne/Hillsdale   ✕ Middle Eastern

The three falafel bars that make up this small chain dot the city—one
on Hawthorne Boulevard, one on NW 21st Avenue, and one in Hillsdale—and (except in Hillsdale) each provides its neighborhood with
a late-night chow spot open until 1:30am on weekdays and until
3am on weekends. The food is good (but not exceptional) and
good for you. Chicken or *kafta* kabob, each served in pita bread,
liven up the menu, which is not particularly extensive—but not
expensive, either. There are several salads to choose from,
and a chicken soup that the kids will love. Can't sleep? Stop
in for a midnight snack of hummus, baba ghanouj, and all
the trimmings alongside the lamb kabob. Beats counting
sheep any day. *Lunch, dinner every day; AE, DIS, MC,
V; no checks; beer and wine.* ♿

GIANT DRIVE-IN

15840 SW Boones Ferry Rd, Lake Oswego
☎ (503) 636-0255
Lake Oswego   ✕ Burgers

The Giant Filler Burger at this 900-square-foot burger joint resembles
a natural wonder—the Grand Canyon with cheese. There are some 30
specialty burgers topped with the likes of soy sauce and pineapple, but
the Filler is the one diagrammed on the company T-shirt: two burgers,
ham, bacon, egg, cheese, and the kitchen sink. Less ambitious
appetites order the Skinny, served with crisp fries and a real ice cream
milk shake: it's like dying and waking up in 1955. And if the thick,
addictive shake isn't enough of a dessert, try the homemade pecan
pie. There is no real drive-in, but takeout is an option. *Lunch, dinner
every day; no credit cards; local checks OK; no alcohol.*

GINO'S RESTAURANT AND BAR

8057 SE 13th Ave
☎ (503) 233-4613
Sellwood   ✕ Italian

What was formerly the Leipzig Tavern—a smoky, dark watering hole
frequented by those more interested in drinking than eating—has
transformed into the delightful Gino's. This is not *au courant* Italian

dining—hip on absolute authenticity, regionalism, or a different kind of pasta every day of the year—but good, old-fashioned Italian-American cooking. Red-and-white checked tablecloths make a perfect backdrop for the fragrant (read "lots of garlic") and hearty food: steamed clams, caesar salad, wonderful garlic bread, and pasta. For the latter, expect generous portions along the traditional meat-and-tomato theme, as well as linguine *vongole* and a ravioli daily special. A $30 dinner for two means you share either the clams or caesar, split a pasta, and choose wine over dessert; but you won't leave the table hungry or dissatisfied. The wine list alone, which features notable producers and remarkable prices, is worth the trip across town. *Lunch Sat only, dinner every day; MC, V; checks OK; full bar.*

GIOVANNI'S ITALIAN RESTAURANT

12390 SW Broadway, Beaverton
☎ *(503) 644-8767*
Beaverton   ✗ *Italian*

If Beaverton has a downtown core, Giovanni's is at the heart of it. Nestled amid the turn-of-the-century buildings on Broadway, Giovanni's is this suburban city's oldest Italian restaurant. Vince and Rose Piscitelli and Mike and Teresa Cortese oversee the family-run business; brother and sister Vince and Teresa opened the restaurant with Giovanni DeNicola (hence the name) in 1975. Giovanni's pride lies in its meaty lasagne, thick-crust pizzas, and a menu full of mouth-watering specialties—rigatoni, fettucine, ravioli, and tortellini. Meatballs, salad dressings, sauces, and pizza crusts are all homemade; you can't miss the delightful aromas wafting into the parking lot. Portions are generous—a "small" 14-inch pizza here, in the $11 to $14 range, easily feeds a family of four, while a large easily satisfies a bigger crowd. The cheerful room, with cozy booths, red-and-white checked tablecloths, and scenes of Italy on the walls, is like home to the many regulars, who

schedule their visits based on the specials (on Mondays a plate of spaghetti, served with garlic bread, antipasto, and soup or salad is only $4.95). Save room for a scoop of spumoni ice cream. *Lunch Mon—Fri, dinner every day; MC, V; checks OK; beer and wine.*

GOLDBERG'S BAKERY

4516 SW Vermont St
☎ (503) 246-4201
Hillsdale
✗ Bakery

You might drop in here for bagels, and that would be a good idea; they're chewy, imperfectly shaped, delicious creations. It probably won't be long, however, before you are seduced by the other breads and baked goods displayed in the glass cases at this longtime, family-owned spot in a little strip mall across from Gabriel Park in southwest Portland. The pizza bagel, topped with a spoonful of garlicky tomato sauce and a cap of mozzarella,. is a savory palm-sized lunch by itself. There are cookies (including luscious macaroons), enormous cinnamon rolls, and authentic challah on Fridays. The bobka is a house specialty. Goldberg's full-service deli, next to the bakery counter, features sandwiches, soups, and salads. One thing you will not find at Goldberg's is that Martha Stewart decorative touch; in fact, the place's functional, dull surroundings have probably not changed much in the 22 years it's been in business. No matter; it's the food that keeps people coming back. In 1998, Goldberg's began selling its wares at the Portland Farmers' Market, seducing Portlanders from all parts of the city; the added exposure, plus the fact that the new southwest Portland swimming, recreation, and community center has been built across the street, may mean busy times ahead. *Breakfast, lunch Tues–Sat; AE, DC, DIS, MC, V; checks OK; no alcohol.* ♿

THE GOLDEN LOAF BAKERY AND DELI

1334 SE Hawthorne Blvd
☎ (503) 231-9758
Hawthorne
✗ Middle Eastern

This sleeper of a deli on Hawthorne offers delicious Middle Eastern fare in a humble setting. An order counter, shelves lined with exotic groceries, and a few tables make up the dining area at this small establishment, where regulars stop in for a falafel lunch on the way to their next appointment. The hummus, baba ghanouj, and tabbouleh are addictive—especially when scooped up with Golden Loaf's own fresh-baked pita bread—and the prices are better than reasonable. For an exotic snack, try the *manaiish*, a pliable, round flatbread rolled with tart spices and sesame seeds, accompanied by a bottle of pomegranate juice. *Lunch, early dinner every day; no credit cards; checks OK; no alcohol.*

GOOD DAY RESTAURANT

312 NW Couch St
(503) 223-1393
Chinatown — *Chinese*

Just around the corner from the China Gate, Good Day features authentic Chinese cuisine; so authentic, perhaps, that some of the menu items may blanch Western palates: pig blood porridge, pork offal, snake soup. Less adventurous diners, however, will be pleased with the Mandarin chicken; mu shu pork and kung pao shrimp; or tasty selections from the "special menu" like honey and garlic spareribs, chicken with orange paste, and five-treasure lettuce roll. Most of the entrees run in the $5 to $7 range and come with the soup of the day (perhaps the fragrant hot and sour soup), tea, and a heaping bowl of steamed rice. Totally unpretentious with a largely Chinese clientele, chopsticks are taken for granted here so you may have to ask for a fork. *Lunch, dinner Wed–Mon; DIS, MC, V; no checks; wine and beer.* ♿

GOOD DOG/BAD DOG

708 SW Alder St
(503) 222-3410
Downtown — *Hot Dogs/Sausage*

A downtown hot dog stand with pedigree, Good Dog/Bad Dog offers a dozen different sausages laden with fried onions in crusty baked rolls. It may be a challenge to your digestive system, but your tongue won't be complaining as you work your way through Oregon smokies, British bangers, garlic sausages, and specials like Louisiana tasso. They're all made inhouse and are undeniably flavorful—if not always fiery. Potato salad, chili, and baked beans can be ordered alongside, as can soda pop or microbrews. Wacky owners and a setting more uptown than ballpark add to this charming mix, a whole new take on man's best friend. *Lunch, early dinner every day; MC, V; checks OK; beer.*

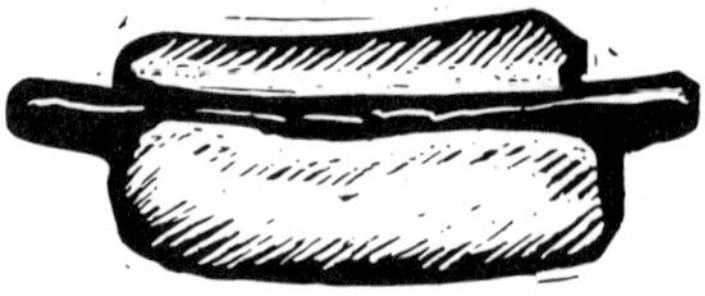

GOOSE HOLLOW INN

1927 SW Jefferson St
☏ *(503) 228-7010*
Goose Hollow   ✕ *Pub Grub*

Somewhere between a cabin and a clubhouse, the warm, well-worn interior and dusty paraphernalia gracing the walls—risqué photos from the last century and indecipherable posters—hint at comfortable old inside jokes. A place where everyone knows your name, the Goose has a loyal and devout following, which accounts for the sensation of stepping into a private party, though you are immedi-

ately made to feel welcome. The quickest way to get drawn into a conversation is to ask about the mustachioed character portrayed in the many posters (indeed it is Bud Clark, former Portland mayor and co-owner of the pub). Proudly advertising itself as a smoking establishment hardly detracts from its popularity, but rather acts as a magnet. Everyone comes here for the Reuben—big, thick, and dripping with Thousand Island—offered in meaty and meatless versions. There are other sandwiches, too, along the lines of roast beef, corned beef, and ham, plus daily soups. Everything is available to go, which makes this a popular late-night stop on the way home. A well-balanced tap board of mostly local micros offers enough choices to please anyone's taste, and when the weather allows there's nothing better than taking that pint outside to the wrap-around deck that sports views of the West Hills and downtown. *Lunch, dinner every day; MC, V; checks OK; beer and wine.*

GOURMET PRODUCTIONS MARKET, FINE FOODS AND CATERING

39 B Ave, Lake Oswego
☏ *(503) 697-7355*
Lake Oswego   ✕ *Deli*

Talk about a niche: This upscale Lake Oswego shop—featuring not just takeout, but also take-home cuisine—is beloved by busy patrons who appreciate high-quality food in the same amount of time it takes to obtain a Whopper and fries. Open weekdays only from 10:30am until 7pm, Gourmet Productions is a one-stop shopping destination for wine, ready-to-eat dinner, and homebaked dessert. That's not to say you can't get a sandwich to eat at one of the four tables: the menu features such luscious varieties as chicken salad—chunks of chicken breast, dried apricot, toasted almonds—on foccacia, or the hot "toasties" (the shop's take on the tuna melt is a favorite among regulars). But many people fax in their orders (503/697-5040) during the afternoon, swing by after work to pick up their bounty, and head home with such exotic entrees as braised lamb shanks or chicken vindaloo. You can always count on a half-dozen or more salads (the nutty japonica, or brown rice, and quinoa salad is flavored with yellow bell peppers, pine nuts, garlic, apricots, and fresh herbs), and about a dozen entrees. Items change with the season's bounty, and every week there's something new. *Lunch, dinner Mon—Fri; MC, V; checks OK; bottles of wine for takeout only.* &

GRAND CENTRAL BAKERY AND CAFE

1444 NE Weidler (and branches)
☎ *(503) 288-1614*
NE Broadway-Lloyd Center/Hawthorne/Multnomah   ✕ *Bakery*

Everyone knows that the secret to making a good sandwich is good bread. Operating on that premise, Grand Central makes some of the best sandwiches in town: Black Forest ham and Swiss on Sour Rye, roasted chicken and cranberry chutney on Como, hummus and tomato on Yeasted Corn. The sack lunch, which includes one of these sandwiches plus a bag of chips, pickle wedge, and cookie, makes for a tasty and reasonably priced meal (it's only a buck over the price of the sandwich). Tables, countertop seating, wine by the glass, and an expanded menu have successfully changed this spot's image from bakery to cafe. In addition to

all the yummy breads and pastries, Grand Central sells marvelous cakes—chocolate, lemon, and carrot—by the slice or to take home whole. *Breakfast, lunch, dinner every day; MC, V; local checks only; beer and wine.* &

THE GYPSY

625 NW 21st Ave
☎ *(503) 796-1859*
Northwest   ✕ *Lounge*

Upon entering the gaudy purple building you may decide you should come back after watching the movie *The Breakfast Club* to identify the clientele. Socialites, jocks, hoods, nerds, and loners linger in the same dimly lit, smoky bar. During the Gypsy's happy hour, from 4pm to 6:30pm Monday through Friday, the entire high school social order (10 years later) is present. They come for the $1.50 beer, discounted well drinks, and half-price food specials; for under $4 you can choose from caesar salad, garlic fries, mozzarella sticks, chicken que- sadillas, burgers, and daily specials like pasta or seafood. Tubes scat- tered throughout the bar and restaurant broadcast vintage cartoons, while the latest and hippest music pumps through the sound system. The wee hours see this funky little bar jump, jive, and gyrate with the same mix of people, while weekend mornings draw the breakfast crowd in for corned beef hash, omelets, and huge pancakes. *Brunch Sat–Sun, lunch, dinner every day; AE, DC, DIS, MC, V; no checks; full bar.* ♿

HANDS ON CAFE

8245 SW Barnes Rd
☎ *(503) 297-1480*
West Hills   ✕ *Inventive Ethnic*

If only every institute of higher learning had a cafeteria like this one. The campus of the Oregon College of Art and Craft may seem an unlikely place to sit down to dazzling baked goods—from scones to multigrain breads to stunning, ever-changing desserts—but the ovens here are as artful as the kilns next door. Low-key lunch and early dinner menus stress salads, soups, and stews, but this is not standard salad- bar fare, with the likes of fresh tuna and pasta salad with capers, cab- bage rolls stuffed with ground veal, and white bean pâté on foccacia adorning the menu. At the popular Sunday brunch, the inspiration ranges from the Pacific Northwest to New Orleans to Peru. Pumpkin bread and bowls of strawberries sprinkled with candied ginger will keep you busy while you wait (and you might have to wait a bit longer than you'd like) for the main course to arrive. *Brunch Sun, lunch Mon–Fri, dinner Mon–Thurs; no credit cards; checks OK; no alcohol.* ♿

HARBORSIDE RESTAURANT AND PILSNER ROOM

0309 SW Montgomery St
☎ *(503) 220-1865*
RiverPlace   ✕ *Happy Hour*

For cheap eats and a view of the Willamette River it's hard to beat the
elegant Harborside Restaurant and Pilsner Room, which becomes a
place of bliss with the addition of their happy hour menu. A $2 drink
purchase entitles you to select from a wide array of
snacks and more substantial offerings, each priced at
$1.95. The menu changes daily and always includes
at least 20 items. Among the staples are soups and
different types of individual pizzas, notably a tangy
barbecue chicken pizza with mozzarella and scallions. Cajun red beans and rice, chicken skewers, and
shredded pork tacos all make for satisfying meals,
and, at less than $2 a plate, you can afford to order
several. With the Full Sail Ale microbrewery just next
door, beer finds its way into the food—like the Pilsner
Room Beer Cheese Soup—and onto the extensive
drink menu. There are 32 beers on tap, including an

impressive list of local microbrews, and a staggering selection of
Northwest wines. Professional types make this their after-work stop,
while the younger set drops in after 9:30pm. *Happy hour daily
4pm–6pm and 9:30pm–close (during summer 10pm–close); AE, DC,
DIS, JCB, MC, V; no checks; full bar.* ♿

HELVETIA TAVERN

10275 NW Helvetia Rd, Hillsboro
☎ *(503) 647-5286*
Hillsboro   ✕ *Pub Grub*

Due west of Portland off Highway 26, a scenic drive that winds
through rolling hills and acres of farms takes you to the only restaurant for miles. Packed with Intel employees, Hillsboro locals, and even
destination diners, people come here for the dependable and juicy
burgers, crispy halibut fish and chips, sandwiches, and thick-cut
French fries. A wooden deck with incredible pastoral views is the draw
in the summer, when many cyclists take to the local roads with only
one thing in mind: the Helvetia Tavern's jumbo burger and a glass of
cold beer. *Lunch, dinner every day; no credit cards; checks OK; beer
and wine.* ♿

HENRY'S CAFE

2508 SE Clinton St
☎ (503) 236-8707
Clinton St

 Cafe

Restaurants are like love affairs—when you least expect it, one comes along and steals your heart. Henry's, a lovely cafe painted in various coffee shades, with lots of dark wood, fir floors, soapstone tables, and a long bar that runs the length of this narrow storefront, is serious crush material. And it's not just another pretty face, either. The breakfast menu satisfies a variety of appetites, from the "Black and White"—two doughnuts and coffee—to the upgraded continental, called "Parisian Brunch" here (French press coffee, a bowl of seasonal fruit, croissant, and jam), and heartier plates like three-egg omelets and potato-vegetable hash. There are only a few choices for lunch—spinach salad, soup du jour, and a handful of sandwiches—but lots of coffeehouse specialties. Whether it's for breakfast or between meals, there's plenty to choose from within the glass case: pastries, zucchini bread, cookies, tortes, and cakes. Probably the most uncanny thing about Henry's is its location; sitting smack-dab in the middle of the Clinton Street neighborhood, a funky mix of vintage stores and slacker eateries, it seems downright upscale. *Breakfast, lunch Tues–Sun; DC, DIS, MC, V; no checks.* ♿

HIGGINS BAR

1239 SW Broadway
☎ (503) 222-9070
Downtown

 Bistro

Though the last decade has brought changes in ownership and venue, from the Broadway Revue to Higgins, the bar here has remained an institution. Maybe it's the location—within a one-block radius of the Performing Arts Center, the Portland Art Museum, and the Oregon History Center—or maybe it's the ghost of spirits past that linger on the liquor-lined wall. Either way, once the acquaintance is made, it's an old friend and a good place to dine on Greg Higgins' creative fare without spending the big bucks. The bistro menu offers some of the same soups and salads served in the dining room of Higgins, as well as a terrific hamburger and house-cured pastrami sandwich with white cheddar—perfect with one of

the beers on tap. A post-work dessert, a single malt Scotch following the symphony, or a burger and a microbrew after a museum visit—no wonder this place is always busy. *Lunch Mon–Fri, dinner every day; AE, DC, DIS, JCB, MC, V; checks OK; full bar.*

HODA'S MIDDLE EASTERN CUISINE

3401 SE Belmont St
☎ *(503) 236-8325*
Belmont   ✕ *Middle Eastern*

Not only does Hoda's make their own pita bread fresh daily, they bake it to order. It comes to the table puffed up like a Chinese lantern, then slowly deflates—meeting its fate with the creamy hummus or the wonderfully smoky baba ghanouj. Given its yeasty aroma and chewy texture, it's tempting to fashion a meal around the pita, but there are other things worth trying as well: the tangy parsley-laden tabbouleh and the tasty *kafta* kabob (skewers of ground beef mixed with intriguing spices) are both delicious. Some items are better than others, with the falafel and Middle Eastern pizzas earning a fair to middling rating, and the clunky spinach pie low on the must-try list (flavorful but too doughy). One of the best bets is the meze for two at $14, but given these low prices, you can also create your own meze by picking and choosing personal favorites from the menu. This space has seen a number of businesses come and go in the last couple years, but Hoda's looks to have some staying power. Whether you eat in the plain, pleasant dining room (fir floors, white walls, metal and vinyl banquet chairs), or get your food to go, you can't help but notice that thanks to Hoda's, this Belmont corner's been seeing a lot of action lately. *Lunch, dinner Mon–Sat; no credit cards; checks OK; no alcohol.*

HOLDEN'S

524 NW 14th Ave
☎ *(503) 916-0099*
Pearl District   ✕ *Cafe*

A huge portrait of Audrey Hepburn keeps watch over this quirky younger sibling of Bima (just around the corner). Originally a market and deli, Holden's has since shape-changed into a deli and cafe. There's a lunchroom feel to what appears to be a purposely unfinished space; help yourself to something to drink from one of the refrigerated cases, order at the counter, then plunk yourself down in a booth. If you're lucky someone will bring out a plate of not-too-huge cinnamon buns or chocolate muffins while you're trying to decide what to order. (Order one.) At lunch time there's soup or chili con carne accompanied by Pearl Bakery bread. For anytime there are sandwiches, Noah's bagels, fruit salad, cookies—you get the picture. If you just feel like hanging out, there are sofas for that, and plenty of tables, too; a spot at the window affords you a front row seat to the happenings on NW 14th Avenue. *Breakfast, lunch, early dinner Mon—Sat; MC, V; no checks; beer and wine.* &

HOLLAND RESTAURANT

1708 Main St, Vancouver, WA
☎ *(360) 694-7842*
Vancouver, WA and Vicinity   ✗ *American*

On a Sunday night in downtown Vancouver the Holland Restaurant is a beacon of light on the otherwise deserted main street. Few care about the motel decor—wallpaper, booths, and fake flowers in shades of pink and teal—or the wall-to-wall carpet and unattractive ceiling tiles (after all, they help keep the place quiet). Instead regulars come here for the good old-fashioned food, ranch-hand portions, great prices, and coffee shop–friendly service. Breakfast, which is served all day, consists of plate-sized omelets in the usual flavors, steak 'n' eggs, and pancakes as big as your head. For lunch and dinner there's the Famous Turkey Dinner—large chunks of freshly roasted bird served with mashed potatoes and gravy—crispy-moist fried chicken, classic sandwiches, and several kinds of hamburgers, including a couple unlikely choices for such a period menu: Garden- and turkey-burgers. Of course there's pie for dessert, along with soda counter favorites: hot fudge sundaes and banana splits piled high with whipped cream, nuts, and a cherry. *Breakfast, lunch, dinner every day; AE, DIS, MC, V; local checks OK; no alcohol.* &

HORN OF AFRICA

3939 NE Martin Luther King Jr. Blvd
☎ *(503) 331-9844*
Northeast, Close In ✗ *East African*

Portland's Ethiopian scene used to be ruled by
Jarra's. And with good reason: the competitors
didn't, well, compete. The dishes here are less spicy
than some at Jarra's, but classics like *doro wat,* a spicy
chicken in red sauce, still have the requisite bite (and
hard-boiled egg). Intriguing lamb and vegetarian
dishes—several kinds of stewed legumes and curried vegetables—show off a range of East African flavors. The food
does not rely wholly on *injera*—the flat, tangy, spongy bread
used to scoop up meat and vegetables—for its starch, and
they serve a rice reminiscent of Armenian pilaf. Gracious,
charming, and politely instructive service makes up for the
practically nonexistent decor. The prices are about half what you'll pay
at Jarra's these days, but this is no Jarra's substitute; the families are
from different regions and cook different but complimentary cuisines.
Imagine that: Portland is a city that has not only a food as exotic as
Ethiopian, but also multiple regional variations therein. Like a "real"
city, it's becoming a burg with choices. *Lunch, dinner Tues–Fri; dinner
only Sat; MC, V; checks OK; no alcohol.* ♿

HOT LIPS PIZZA

1909 SW 6th Ave (and branch)
☎ *(503) 224-0311*
Downtown/Raleigh Hills ✗ *Pizza*

You'll have plenty of choices for toppings at this longtime-favorite
pizzeria: sun-dried tomatoes, Montrachet, Oregon blue cheese, fresh
garlic, herbs soaked in olive oil, myriad sausages, and good old pepperoni. There are about 40 toppings to add to pies already heavenly
with lots of cheese, just enough housemade sauce, and a soft-and-
chewy hand-thrown crust. Hot Lips does enough business in by-the-
slice sales—after all, what do college students live on?—that it can
usually offer a selection of four or five varieties. Besides the downtown
location near PSU, there's a suburban branch in Raleigh Hills (4825
SW 76th Avenue, 503/297-8424). *Lunch, dinner every day; AE, DIS,
MC, V; local checks only; beer and wine (downtown only).* ♿

HOYT STREET CAFE

1131 NW Hoyt St
☎ *(503) 226-3451*
Pearl District ✗ *American*

You can order lunch or dinner at this spacious, new Pearl District neighborhood restaurant, but given the constraints of this book (cheap, remember?), we can't recommend that you do. However, when breakfast is a relative bargain, is served all day long, and tastes as good as this does, there's no need to look further. Egg options and a variety of omelets head the list, but there's also French toast (made with brioche) and homemade granola. Ron Baldwin, formerly a chef at nearby Paragon, and his wife, Paula, opened Hoyt Street Cafe in 1998. Their restaurant sits on the corner of NW Hoyt and 12th Avenue—on the edge of the Pearl's thriving gallery scene. Besides the food and location, there's another feature we espe- cially like: unlike most places to get breakfast in northwest Portland, Hoyt Street Cafe can accom- modate large parties—from the littlest family mem- bers, who enjoy the diversion of crayons and white paper on every table (especially appropriate for a restaurant in this arty part of town, don't you think?), to elders, who appreciate the good coffee, the range of egg dishes, and, frankly, the crayons, too. *Breakfast every day; MC, V; checks OK; beer and wine.* ♿

ICHIBAN

13599 NW Cornell Rd, Cedar Hills
☎ *(503) 641-0331*
West Hills ✗ *Japanese*

Warning: Eat sushi at Ichiban and you will not eat cheap. This strip-mall Japanese restaurant can get pricey if you have a one-track mind for raw fish. On the other hand, combination plates offer good value and variety: tempura, teriyaki, yakisoba, barbecue, or a California roll all come with miso soup, steamed rice, pickles, and a salad. Including sushi or sashimi on your combo plate will cost you more, as will choosing three items. You can also order a la carte, but do so carefully: the bill adds up quickly if you don't pay attention. Ichiban is relatively kid-friendly and has items on the menu to convert even wary children. In addition to the standard Japanese fare, there are some Korean offerings, like spicy soup, barbecued beef, and homemade *kim chee*.

Lunch, dinner Mon–Fri, dinner only Sat; AE, MC, V; no checks; beer, wine, and sake. ♿

IKENOHANA
14308 SW Allen Blvd, Beaverton
☎ *(503) 646-1267*
Beaverton ✗ *Japanese*

The suburban strip-mall storefront opens into a modest space (with a tiny sushi bar in one corner) where Japanese paper screens and lanterns give a private and charming feel, and even when things are busy, it's not noisy. The menu allows a wide range of options, from sushi and sashimi to tempura, katsu dishes, teriyaki, and noodles. You can't go wrong here: the sashimi is elegantly presented and very fresh and firm. A

plentiful plate of sushi includes wonderful mackerel and eel. Even the simple yakisoba noodles are spicy and cooked just right. If you look like you don't know how to mix the wasabi and soy sauce for the sushi, the friendly waitstaff will show you. *Lunch Mon–Fri, dinner every day; MC, V; no checks; beer and wine.* ♿

INDIA OVEN
3862 SE Hawthorne Blvd
☎ *(503) 872-9687*
Hawthorne ✗ *Indian*

What was formerly the first floor of the Hawthorne Masonic Temple is now the sparsely and frugally decorated dining room of the India Oven. While the decor—comprised of cheap chandeliers, a 3-foot long fluorescent light, and a row of Indian-themed pictures along the walls—lacks both imagination and capital investment, the food shines. Mr. Samra and his family graciously invite you to enjoy the foods of their kitchen, starting with the crispy (but not greasy) samosas filled with potatoes, peas, coriander, and mustard seed. Other dishes worth trying from the vegetarian-friendly menu include *palak paneer* (spinach sautéed with Indian cheese), lentil dal, and a selection of *naan* (flatbread baked in the clay oven). For nonvegetarians, the moist tandoori chicken and chicken *mahkanwala* (chicken in a creamy sauce spiced with cumin and coriander) make excellent entrees. To sample a range of what's available; try the lunch buffet: all you can eat for $5.95, served daily from 11am to 2:30pm. *Lunch, dinner every day; AE, DIS, MC, V; checks OK; beer and wine.* ♿

J + M CAFE
537 SE Ash St
☎ *(503) 230-0463*
Southeast, Close In ✕ *Breakfast*

The high-ceilinged brick room, partitioned with walls painted an elegant green, is full of entertaining details: an intriguing painting of multicolored squares, a huge oak cooler, an old-fashioned lunch counter, a women's restroom key that hangs from a foot-long rubber alligator, and a coffee station where you can fill up in the tacky mug of your choice (Doubletree Inns? Carnation cocoa?). But the atmo isn't the only thing you'll savor; the menu has enough variety and quality to hold your interest for repeat visits. Try the breakfast burrito—black beans, scrambled eggs, and cheddar cheese in all the right proportions, rolled into a flour tortilla and topped with sour cream, olives, and fresh salsa. The J + M Plate is a toasted English muffin topped with bacon, basted eggs, fontina, cheddar, *and* Parmesan. For lighter appetites there is 10-grain cereal sprin-

kled with currants, granola with dried cranberries, or a Belgian cornmeal waffle. Latecomers be warned: although breakfast is served until 2pm during the week, only four breakfast  items are served throughout the lunch hour on those days. But there are also sandwiches, soups, and salads. *Breakfast every day, lunch Mon—Fri; no credit cards; checks OK; beer and champagne.*

JAKE'S GRILL
611 SW 10th Ave
☎ *(503) 220-1850*
Downtown ✕ *Happy Hour*

The truth is, you really can't go wrong with a menu where every item is less than $2. If you don't like your first choice, just order something else. At Jake's Grill, the happy hour bar menu, served in the late afternoon and late-night hours seven days a week, epitomizes cheap eats—every item is just $1.95. Located in the upscale, gorgeously renovated Governor Hotel, Jake's Grill, opened in 1994, is the most recent addition to the McCormick and Schmick's family of dining establishments in Portland. While the dining room side of Jake's Grill offers pricey (but well worth it) renditions of lamb chops, steaks, and signature M&S seafood dishes, the bar strives for economical and consistent. The happy hour menu changes every few months with some items, cheeseburgers in particular,  holding fast. Sautéed mushrooms, teriyaki chicken wings, fancy quesadillas, and seafood cocktails are typically featured. The only requirement is that you order a drink for a minimum of $2, which should not be a problem considering the full bar and the lineup of Northwest wines and microbrews. The atmosphere here could be called Portland saloon—jeans and T-shirt–clad customers are likely to be spotted grabbing a cheap, early dinner at one table while a black tie couple savors a pre-opera drink and a bite to eat at the next. Despite the fact that Jake's Grill is still a baby of a restaurant when compared to its century-old sibling, Jake's Crawfish, located just a few blocks away, the Grill's happy hour secret is definitely out—so it may be difficult to get a table. And, once you're seated, expect to do some serious secondhand smoking. *Happy hour every day(4pm–6pm); AE, DC, DIS, MC, V; no checks; full bar.* &

JAMIE'S

838 NW 23rd Ave
☎ *(503) 248-6784*
Northwest   *Burgers*

If the family's on the prowl for a decent one-third pound burger (or twice that size, if you request it), a real milk shake served with a pouf of whipped cream on top, and a little distraction in the form of '50s tunes on the jukebox, this may be your spot. A minichain, with restaurants in Eugene, Corvallis, and Portland, Jamie's succeeds because of its quality: the food is 10 times better than anything you'll get at a fast-food chain. The menu is extensive—there are 17 choices of burgers (Rosy's, with salsa and avocado, is a favorite) and as many sandwiches—and the ice cream in that Black Cow is the real thing. While adults might wish the atmosphere were a little warmer—with a little less goofy nostalgia—kids adore it, especially the coin-operated cars. *Breakfast, lunch, dinner every day; AE, MC, V; no checks; beer only.* &

JARRA'S ETHIOPIAN RESTAURANT

1435 SE Hawthorne Blvd
☎ (503) 230-8990
Hawthorne   ✗ Ethiopian

Several Ethiopian restaurants have appeared in Portland over the years, but Jarra's is still the place to get into an explosive, sweat-inducing Abyssinian stew. This is the restaurant to teach you what's *wat*: made with chicken, lamb, or beef, the *wat* (stews) are deep red, oily, and packed with peppery after-kicks. Full dinners come with assorted stewed meats and vegetables, all permeated with vibrant spices and mounded on *injera*—the spongy Ethiopian bread that doubles as plate and fork. Tucked into the bottom of an old Portland home, this is the neighborhood's unequaled heat champ. *Dinner Tues–Sat; MC, V; checks OK; full bar.* ♿

JOHN STREET CAFE

8338 N Lombard St
☎ (503) 247-1066
St. Johns   ✗ American

Though urban renewal is on the way—why else would Starbucks open another coffee shop here?—this small community on the northern edge of Portland looks a lot like it did circa 1950. A bright spot in this sometimes quaint, sometimes desolate land-scape (depending on the day, density of cloud cover, and one's frame of mind) is John Street Cafe. Run by the former owners of Tabor Hill Cafe on Hawthorne Boulevard, this cafe possesses many of the same winning qualities: congenial service, an eclectic collection of drawings and paintings that color the walls, and an element of pleasant earthiness. Add to that the personality of its corner space—  high ceilings, tall windows, polished concrete floors—it has a lightness even when the sun's not out. The cafe is only open for breakfast and lunch, and both meals offer favorites such as seasonal pancakes; a fresh fruit cup perked up with chopped hazelnuts, dried fruit, and sweetened yogurt; omelets large enough to share (the service charge to split it is well worth it given the extra roasted potatoes and toast added to each plate); and old-fashioned sandwiches made better by the quality of the ingredients. Try one of the hamburgers, a Reuben, or the cafe's twist on the BLT, the TAB—sliced turkey breast with avocado and bacon. There are also several pasta dishes for lunch, as well as soup, salads, and specials of the day. *Breakfast, lunch Wed–Sun; MC, V; local checks; no alcohol.* ♿

JUNIOR'S CAFE

1742 SE 12th Ave
☎ *(503) 235-5474*
Southeast, Close In   🍴 *Breakfast*

When owners Kurt Van Vlack and Monica and Jennifer Ransdell tried serving breakfast at their first-born Dots Cafe, they found it just wasn't meant to be. It was too dark for any save the most hardened alcoholics and moles to rightfully start their day in. Their solution was to open Junior's, a smaller, lighter space on 12th Avenue just south of Hawthorne Boulevard. The menu picks up the breakfast ball and runs with it, turning out a Greek scramble with garlic, spinach, feta, and savory chicken sausage, perfect fluffy waffles (though these can be disappointingly small), and heaps of salty potatoes with paprika. The few lunch items include homemade soups, spinach salad with toasted almonds and fresh Parmesan cheese, and a delicious pork loin sandwich with a garlic-horseradish mayo and roasted red peppers. Sometimes the wait can be long, and as you look around traces of a late night can be found on surrounding faces. The panacea: a fresh-squeezed grapefruit mimosa. *Breakfast, lunch Wed–Mon; no credit cards; checks OK; mimosas only.* ♿

JUSTA PASTA COMPANY

1336 NW 19th Ave
☎ *(503) 229-0646*
Northwest   *Italian*

Pasta lovers rave about Roland Carfagno's takeout/retail shop: not only can you stop in for a hearty pasta box lunch, you can buy first-rate fresh ravioli to take home for dinner at the same time. Choose one of the ravioli specials—maybe chicken sausage, three-cheese, or roasted potato and Parmesan—then pick one of the four sauces on the menu (such as roasted pepper cacciatore). Bravo! You've got a feast. Even if you're not a pasta lover, check it out; despite the place's name there's always a soup and salad. All menu items are under $7; a good half are less than $5. And, with a recent expansion there are now about 25 seats; a vast improvement

over the few coveted stools. The tidy warehouse location near the corner of NW 19th Avenue and Pettygrove Street may look from the outside like it might house an auto repair shop, but rest assured, inside all that's being fixed is food. *Lunch Mon–Sat; AE, MC, V; checks OK; no alcohol.* &

KEN'S HOME PLATE
1852 SE Hawthorne Blvd
☎ *(503) 236-9520*
Hawthorne ✗ *Inventive Ethnic*

Is your wallet too thin to support your haute cuisine inclinations? Dragging home in the pouring rain after a long day? Ken's Home Plate, a recent addition to the vibrant Hawthorne food scene, is a delicious respite from the daily dinner grind.

Chef-owner Ken Gordon prepares 12 to 14 outstanding entrees daily—interesting, well-executed, and authentic dishes from around the globe, prepared on the premises and ready to heat and serve in the privacy of your own home. Gordon's skill and use of high-quality ingredients are  evident in the *bastilla* (Moroccan chicken pie), highly seasoned Tuscan meat loaf, heavenly spinach lasagne with four cheeses, and chicken pot pie, to name but a few of the dozens of dishes in his repertoire. The many excellent entrees may be ordered a la carte or, for $6.75 to $8.50, with your choice of an accompanying side dish or salad. For dessert, the bittersweet chocolate pudding is a specialty. Ken's takeout menu changes daily, with a few standards (stuffed chicken breasts) usually available. If you prefer to stay, there are a few tables for sit-down diners in the spare but inviting storefront. Ken's also caters a wide range of events, small or large, and with advance notice can prepare a special takeout meal for a crowd. *Lunch, dinner Tues–Sat; MC, V; checks OK; beer and wine.* &

KING BURRITO
2924 N Lombard St
☎ *(503) 283-9757*
North Portland ✗ *Mexican*

Fluorescent lighting, plants in 5-gallon plastic buckets, and a jukebox packed with Selena singles sets the tone at this burrito joint, which seems to be run by 18-year-old boys in baggy jeans. King Burrito is unassuming, gritty, and jammed with satisfied customers grooving on food so good and cheap it's tempting to give the cashier a little more than he asks for. Burritos, of course, make up the bulk of the menu, which is a carnivore's dream (*carne asada, steak picado, al pastor*) but considerate of vegetarians as well *(chiles rellenos,* veggie chimichanga). Nonburrito items such as the Special Quesadilla, a flat tortilla sandwich filled with chicken, green chiles, and avocado, or soft tacos, corn tortillas wrapped around seasoned meat, cilantro, and onion, are equally inexpensive and fresh. For customers who crave *menudo,* the traditional Mexican tripe soup, they can get their fix here on weekends, while the pleasure of sipping *horchata—*a sweet and milky almond drink laced with cinnamon—can be had any time of the week. King Burrito does not serve what most think of as breakfast. However, it opens at 10am every morning and even earlier on the weekends (unofficially), offering the same menu to accommodate the breakfast habits of customers who like a hearty first meal of the day. *Early lunch, dinner every day; AE, DIS, MC, V; no checks; no alcohol.*

KORNBLATT'S DELICATESSEN

628 NW 23rd Ave
☎ *(503) 242-0055*
Northwest   ✗ *Deli*

Huge breakfasts, skyscraper sandwiches, pickles on the table—these are the things the neighborhood locals love about Kornblatts's. Add to that list chewy, determined bagels that come in mind-bending—blueberry cinnamon?—as well as satisfyingly predictable (the super onion,

which warms to the excellent smoked fish) varieties, and you begin to understand the success of a place notorious for its bad service. Forceful chopped liver, pungent corned beef, cabbage borscht, blintzes, and kugel are also on the menu, as well as pot roast with latkes. *Breakfast, lunch, dinner every day; MC, V; checks OK; beer, wine, and select liquor.* ♿

L'AUBERGE BISTRO

2601 NW Vaughn St
☎ (503) 223-3302
Northwest   ✖ Bistro

Stepping into L'Auberge is like traveling back in time 25 years—when
revamped houses set the stage for fine dining, cane and chrome chairs
were all the rage, and a restaurant's cutting-edge art consisted of the
occasional framed nude. Add to this setting
a warm fireplace in the winter, a cool deck in
the summer, the best sidecars in town, and
well-executed food, and you begin to understand why even '70s-phobes make the
L'Auberge bar one of their haunts. Unlike the
restaurant, which serves a formal prix fixe
French menu, the bar specializes in classic
bistro fare at friendly prices. Choose several
dishes to share in the $10 and under range—
pâté, mixed greens, a plate of imported cheeses, steamed clams, *coq au
vin*, or one of the enticing sandwiches—for a perfectly satisfying meal.
Desserts are also worth noting, especially the fresh fruit tarts and
renowned poached lemon cheesecake. *Lunch Mon–Fri, dinner every
day; AE, DC, DIS, MC, V; local checks only; full bar.*

L'IL MEXICO RESTAURANT

5827 E Burnside St
☎ (503) 231-6618
Laurelhurst   ✖ Central American

This lively establishment on E Burnside Street and 59th Avenue is more
Guatemalan in heritage and cuisine than its name suggests. Romeo
and Rosa Muñoz started their restaurant back when Guatemalan food
was totally foreign to Portland, and worked their native specialties into
the menu alongside familiar Mexican dishes. Lucky for us! You'd be
hard pressed to order the same thing twice here—the menu is extensive
and inviting. Traditional meat preparations are emphasized more than
taqueria fare, although tacos, burritos, tostadas, and tamales are also
available, and very good. Mexican dinners include chicken mole and
carnitas, as well as the less-familiar *pastor* (marinated pork) and *steak
picado* (peppered, sliced beef steak). Guatemalan dinners, offered at
$7.75, include *jocon* (chicken in a green tomato sauce), *carne guisada*
(beef broiled with tomato, green tomato, and pumpkin seed), and the
incredible Banana Leaf Tamale. Also worth trying: *kaquik*, a thick

Guatemalan turkey soup, or one of several shrimp specialties of the house. Pickings are slim when it comes to vegetarian entrees, a point made obvious by the choice of *seven* meat fillings for the burritos. The festive dining room often fills with neighborhood regulars, who also appreciate the relaxed, friendly service and a variety of Mexican and American beers and margaritas from the adjoining lounge. *Lunch, dinner every day; AE, DC, DIS, MC, V; checks OK; full bar.* &

LA BUCA

2309 NW Kearney St
☎ *(503) 279-8040*
Northwest   ✕ *Italian*

In a part of town best known for its upscale eateries, La Buca stands apart as a place to get uncomplicated pastas, panini, and salads, all at prices that respect a slacker's budget. The "bread spreads"—sun-dried tomato; basil; and, our fave, the salty, savory olive—are, at $1.25 each, a very affordable appetizer. Slathered on a slice of the bread (made by Grand Central Baking Company), a selection of spreads could almost fill you up. But save room for one of the eight or nine pastas, such as the penne puttenesca or the simple spaghetti with garlic and red pepper flakes. The house salad of greens tossed with slivers of red onion is topped with a balsamic vinaigrette (two can share a large salad handily); spinach and caesar salads are also available. The soup of the day might be a creamy tomato, and the mashed potatoes with pesto is a favorite of many regulars. Wine—a half-dozen reds and a lone Pinot Grigio—is available by the glass; refills on sodas are free. The crowd at La Buca consists of people of all ages, but the photos of rock stars decorating the bright walls give the place away as a twenty-something hangout. Word to the wise: La Buca is nestled in the corner of a diminutive strip mall deep in the heart of northwest Portland—but well worth the hunt. At press time there were rumors about a new La Buca East, to be opened on the corner of NE 28th Avenue and Couch. *Lunch, dinner Mon—Sat, dinner only Sun; MC, V; checks OK; beer and wine.* &

LA CALACA COMELONA

1408 SE 12th Ave
☎ *(503) 239-9675*
Southeast, Close In   ✗ *Mexican*

As proud owner Patricia Cabrera boasts, burritos are what they do *not* make at "The Hungry Skeleton," a brightly painted cantina crammed with rustic wooden furniture, suspended skeletons, and Frida Kahlo and Diego Rivera reproductions.

Behind the scenes at this colorful establishment, the kitchen turns out its own tortillas, *chorizo* sausage, and daily salsas. What this means for those who sup here: knock-your-socks-off tacos (try the oven-roasted pork and pineapple). Your choice of grilled steak, *chorizo*, or chicken can also be wrapped into a taco, featured on a combination plate, or worked into a quesadilla. Veg-

etarians can feast on the *sopa*: a pillow of masa topped with queso fresco, lettuce, tomatoes, onion, guacamole, and sour cream. There are also fresh (as in made-to-order) juices, including the "Oasis," a tantalizing concoction made with oranges and cactus juice. Also on the beverage list are cinnamon-laced hot chocolate, and—it was only a matter of time—margaritas. *Lunch, dinner Tues–Sat, dinner only Mon; DC, MC, V; checks OK; beer, wine, and margaritas.* ♿

LA CRUDA

2500 SE Clinton St
☎ *(503) 233-0745*
Clinton St   ✗ *Mexican*

It means "the hangover" in Spanish, but don't wait for the "morning after" to come in: La Cruda's a smart place to start the evening. Just off the funky crossroads of Clinton Street and SE 26th Avenue, amidst coffeehouses and vintage shops, La Cruda feels like two restaurants in one—cafe up front, cantina in the back. The cooks here dish up monumental burritos with a choice of fillings wrapped in one of four types of tortillas—flour, roasted tomato, spinach, or chipotle pepper. There are tacos, tortilla soup, enchiladas (including a spicy rock shrimp version that has quite a following), and quesadillas. A trip to the salsa bar livens up everything; there are usually five choices along the lines of a zesty red, a tamer verde, a refreshing pico de gallo, a no-holds-barred chipotle, and, best of all, a sweet and spicy pineapple. The place has a comfy quality—furnishings are as retro as the hipsters who hang here—and you'll find a lot of reasons to come back: great margaritas, plentiful sides of fresh chips and guacamole, and a scintillating jalapeño-pumpkin ice cream. And, if you do have a hangover (the bar in back stays open until 2am), they make a yummy plate of breakfast tacos and a mean Bloody Mary. *Breakfast Sat–Sun; lunch, dinner every day; AE, MC, V; checks OK; full bar.* &

LA SIRENITA

2817 NE Alberta St
☏ *(503) 335-8283*
Alberta St   ✗ *Mexican*

The lure of La Sirenita proves too strong for the dozens of locals, artists, families, and business people who lunch on Alberta Street. Regulars line up daily for some of the best burritos, tacos, and tamales in town. Although it has suffered through several remodels in the past few years, including both expansions and contractions, the spirit of La Sirenita's food and its patrons remains intact. Here laborers lunch alongside urban renewal project managers, and babies in highchairs rub elbows with Alberta Street artists. All food is made to order and served on cafeteria trays. Fresh, distinct flavors dominate (no refrieds here), and servings are generous. Super burritos are the standouts; each comes with a choice of chicken, beef, pork, *carnitas*, beef tongue, or vegetarian filling, and a surprise *chile relleno* inside. At $2.75, this is one of the best lunches around. Tacos, tamales, and que-

sadillas, all with a choice of meat (or without) will not disappoint. La Sirenita's house specialties all focus on seafood: *Caldo Siete Mars* (Seven Seas Soup), shrimp and octopus cocktail, shrimp tostadas, and shrimp soup. Cheeseburgers are a fairly recent addition, and worth every cent. Top off your meal with a Tamarindo, an ice-cold tamarind juice drink, or *horchata*, a milky-white sweet rice drink. Other Mexican and American soft drinks are also available. *Lunch, dinner every day; no credit cards; no checks; no alcohol.* &

LANAI CAFE

3145 SE Hawthorne Blvd
☎ *(503) 239-4857*
Hawthorne   ✗ *Vietnamese*

Though only as big as two college dorm rooms smooshed together and tattered on the edges, Lanai Cafe offers food that lifts you beyond the wanting decor, permanently-stained tablecloths, ringing telephone, and downright cold temperatures during winter months (bring a warm sweater). Start with the tofu sour soup, and you'll wonder if anything else can measure up. It can. Skip the greasy egg rolls, though, and concentrate on the entrees: five-spice or ginger chicken, beef satays, and pan-fried noodles (with shrimp, beef, or chicken—all yummy). The tongue-tingling five-spice chicken—flavored with cinnamon, mango, coconut, garlic, and sesame—is particularly good cold, straight out of the carton the next day, if you like that sort of thing. Consistently polite service and free meal delivery (with a $20 minimum order to southeast and northeast neighborhoods) land this spot on the repeat list. *Lunch, dinner Mon—Sat; MC, V; no checks; no alcohol.*

LAURELTHIRST PUBLIC HOUSE

2958 NE Glisan St
☎ *(503) 232-1504*
Laurelhurst   ✗ *Pub Grub*

If it were located near a college campus, this is the kind of place people would simply call "home." Tavern by night, cafe by day, there's always someone hanging out here, either noshing on a late morning breakfast, playing pool with a pitcher, or listening to music into the wee hours. A beautiful antique bar and comfortable leather booths make for a worn-in, cozy setting; when it's not live it's probably Bob Dylan or Buddy Holly in the background. Some would call the fare classic hangover food—unpretentious and filling—and both breakfast and lunch are served from 9am to 3pm daily. The kitchen turns out a noteworthy plate of home fries, especially good with cheddar cheese,  salsa, and sour cream. There are also biscuits and gravy (sausage or vegetarian), thick slices of French toast, omelets and scrambles. Toasted bread bowls filled with homemade soup or chili, sandwiches, salads, and veggieburgers round out the lunch menu, with highlights like the Garden of Sin Veggieburger (with bacon!). The evening into late-night menu offers many of the lunch dishes, with additions like foccacia and nachos. With microbrews on tap and good, strong coffee any time of the day, it's no surprise that neighbors often stop in. *Breakfast, lunch, late night menu every day; MC, V; no checks; beer and wine.* ♿

LE BISTRO MONTAGE
301 SE Morrison St
☎ *(503) 234-1324*
Southeast, Close In   ✕ *Cajun*

It may come as a surprise that Portland's definitively hip late-night hangout is open for lunch; you won't get the 2am energy, but you'll get the same unexpectedly good, cheap Southern/Cajun cuisine. (When Montage says spicy, it's not kidding.) If you join the later

crowd, you may have to wait for a spot at one of the long tables for such Cajun specialties as Spicy Mac (glorified macaroni with Cajun gravy, jalapeños, tomatoes, and Parmesan); blackened snapper; or jambalaya topped with crab, rabbit sausage, or alligator meat. Dinners

are both ambitious and unique—from spicy frogs' legs to alligator pâté to green eggs and Spam. Round out your meal with a slice of pecan pie. The loud hum of conversation and music is punctuated with waiters' shouts to the open kitchen announcing shooters—either an oyster or mussel served in a shot glass. Lots of wines are offered by the glass and are promptly refilled in jelly jar–like vessels with a nod in the right direction. The topnotch and often snarky waiters manage to look as if they're having as good a time as most of the guests. *Lunch Mon–Fri, dinner every day; no credit cards; checks OK; beer, wine, and select liquor.* ♿

LEAF AND BEAN CAFE
4936 NE Fremont St
☎ *(503) 281-1090*
Alameda-Beaumont   ✕ *Cafe*

From the warm palette of the walls to the cashier's smile, the atmosphere of this neighborhood cafe makes you feel at home—especially if you're vegetarian. The Leaf and Bean offers lots of healthy choices and blends fabulous flavors into the mostly vegetarian menu. Every day brings three different soups, always two vegan and one vegetarian, as well as fresh, crisp salads (try the delicious baby greens with feta, walnuts, and pickled red onions). Sandwiches, too, are a real treat, with standouts like the hearty Mediterranean Chicken, loaded up with roasted red peppers, kalamata olives, feta cheese, and capers. Or go for the Avo-Vegetarian: avocado, cream cheese, cucumbers, walnuts, and red onion, heaped between two slices of pane di Como slathered with an olive-caper mayo. Whether you want to meet friends for lunch or grab a cup of joe and read the paper, it's a nice stop off the beaten path. On weekends breakfast consists of potato scrambles (your choice of eggs or tofu), frittatas, and waffles. *Breakfast, lunch Sat–Sun; lunch, early dinner Mon–Fri, no credit cards; checks OK; no alcohol.* &

LITTLE WING CAFE
529 NW 13th Ave
☎ *(503) 228-3101*
Pearl District   ✕ *Soup/Salad/Sandwich*

Given this alleyway cafe's popularity with the Pearl District's lunch crowd, come noon it's hard to find a spot at one of the Formica tables. Standard lunch items (soup, salad, sandwiches) are gussied up with interesting and fresh ingredients, and all the sandwiches are served on Grand Central bread. Daily specials exhibit the kitchen's creativity; you might find a portobello mushroom burger or lemongrass chicken. In 1999 the cafe started serving dinner, which features a lot of the sandwiches from the lunch menu, as well as entrees like turkey brisket with mashed potatoes and lemon Dijon chicken. Specials and entrees push the budget envelope; set your sights on some of the heartier sandwiches or a smattering of appetizers  for a casual meal. Afterwards, there are cookies (when the business first opened it was called "The Little Italian Cookie Company" and those are the kind of cookies you'll find here). *Lunch Mon–Sat; MC, V; checks OK; no alcohol.*

LORN AND DOTTIE'S LUNCHEONETTE

322 SW 2nd Ave
☎ (503) 221-2473
Downtown   ✖ Diner

This clean, well-lighted space might surprise you on your first visit—
especially if you're expecting a casual luncheonette. At Lorn and
Dottie's, situated on the edge of Old Town, brass nameplates mark
the booths of regulars, the waiter wears a bow tie, and hot coffee is
poured with the frequency of FedEx planes taking off and landing. A
basic eggs, ham, and toast breakfast is actually eggs, several slices of
Canadian ham, savory potato pancakes served alongside a dish of
applesauce, and a thick slice of cinnamon bread (or jalapeño corn
bread or banana nut bread—or, of course, basic toast). Though you
might be taken aback by the prices— nearly $8 for the breakfast just
described—you may not eat again until supper. But be of good cheer,
there are also plenty of items priced around $6. Regulars like the
Italian eggs, with sausage and Parmesan, or the decadent apple pancake. Friday is Zoom day: a bowl of the toothsome hot cereal goes for
$3.95. Lorn and Dottie's is open until 2pm weekdays, with a variety of
sandwiches served at lunch, but on the weekends breakfast is the only
meal available. *Breakfast every day, lunch Mon–Fri; MC, V; no checks;
no alcohol.* ♿

LOS 3 HERMANOS

SE Division St, between 33rd and 34th Avenues
☎ (no phone)
SE Division   ✖ Mexican

One of the true joys of a city like Portland is finding a place you
wouldn't touch with a 10-foot pole in a huge metropolis that yields
one of the freshest, most authentic,
and least expensive meals in town.
This lunch wagon parked in the lot of
the old Ichidai, now Kappaya, restaurant is run by young women who
speak nary a word of English. The
menu includes tacos and burritos of

tripas (tripes or intestines) and *cabeza* (brains) as well as other more
familiar varieties—savory pork *carnitas*, exquisite beef *pastor*, hearty
lamb *birria*, and lime-drenched shrimp ceviche. Everything is served on
a paper plate with a rough radish, fresh cilantro, and a lime wedge,
and goes for a dollar a pop. For beverages, there are bottles of

Mexican soda, with flavors like Mandarin orange or guava. Take the food to go, or if you choose to "dine in," there are plastic tables and chairs on the gravel parking lot with an umbrella to ward off the rain. *Lunch, dinner every day; no credit cards; no checks; no alcohol.*

LOW BROW LOUNGE
1036 NW Hoyt St
☎ *(503) 226-0200*
Pearl District   ✗ *Lounge*

The cavernous feel of the Low Brow Lounge is both cozy and sleazy-cool. A dark, smoky interior and the large, vinyl booths attract hipsters and late-nighters. The menu, a cross between deli and mom's kitchen, includes choices such as creamy mac 'n' cheese accompanied by an upscale salad of mesclun greens or Guinness stew, hearty meat loaf served with garlic mashed potatoes and maple green beans; roasted turkey sandwich with crispy tater tots or fries; and a Gardenburger with a special horseradish sauce and a choice of fries or tots. The fries are crispy, and the tots are reminiscent of the ones mom served with fish sticks in 1978. (A side of these treasures from the past will only cost you $2.50, and the memories evoked are complimentary.) The staff is mellow and courteous, and food and drinks are delivered in a timely manner. Happy hour spans from 5pm to 7pm every day, and features $1 off of all pints and well drinks. The Low Brow keeps late hours so that Portland's night crawlers and restaurant folk have a place to relax in the wee morning hours. *Lunch, dinner Mon–Sat; AE, DIS, MC, V; no checks; full bar.* &

MACHEEZMO MOUSE
723 SW Salmon St (and branches)
☎ *(503) 228-3491*
Downtown/SW Macadam/NE Broadway-Lloyd Center/
Portland Airport/Tigard   ✗ *Mexican*

Stepping into the Salmon Street Macheezmo Mouse is like entering a time warp back to the era when Bon Jovi ruled the airwaves. This is not some sort of hip, retro reinterpretation of the early '80s, mind you, this is the real McCoy in all its bombastic splendor: primary colors, anodized aluminum, giant Lichtenstein-inspired murals, and sections of a life-sized single-seater airplane suspended over the cavernous inner dining area. Just as all of this used to be on the cutting edge, so too was the concept for food—healthy Mexican fast food. Today Portlanders seem to have grown tired of their once-favorite Mouse—the effects of too much Boss sauce?—and a few of the original eateries, namely those on NW 23rd Avenue and on Hawthorne Boulevard, have closed shop. That said, Mouse fans heartily and heart-smartily (calorie counts and cholesterol info are all part of the package) approve of efforts to enliven the menu with new flavors. In addition to the original burritos, tacos, and salads, there are such things as the Thai burrito, a delicious fusion of flavors bursting with snap peas, fresh cabbage, and peanut sauce. Though some may shudder at the concept, others succumb, faithful to the Mouse creed: "Fresh, fit, fast." *Lunch, dinner every day; DC, DIS, MC, V; checks OK; beer only.*

MAGPIE CAFE

4823 N Lombard St
☎ *(503) 240-4789*
North Portland ✗ *Cafe*

Quietly nestled among the eclectic shops of North Lombard, Magpie Cafe offers the chance to visit Grandma's house, but without the emotional baggage. Regulars do, however, become fond of the warm, cheerful proprietor, Mary Ellen, and to her homemade soup and bread and cozy decor. From the pictures of magpies to the colorful wooden fish suspended from the ceiling, there's plenty to look at while you wait for your meal. Mary Ellen's home cookin' means baked potatoes stuffed with broccoli and cheese; chicken with Indonesian peanut sauce, rice, and veggies; tortellini with sweet potatoes and herbs; and Tuscan white bean soup—all for less than $4 each. Most food is prepared ahead of time and reheated to order, which means it's hot and quick to the table. The weekend breakfast menu includes poached eggs, pancakes, quiche, and breakfast potato dishes. Though the coffee isn't strong, at 75 cents a cup it's hardly worth knocking. *Breakfast, lunch Tues—Thurs and Sat—Sun; no credit cards; checks OK; no alcohol.* ♿

MAMA'S CORNER CAFE

14035 SE Stark St
☎ *(503) 257-2753*
Southeast, Beyond 39th *Breakfast*

Though it's called Mama's, it's actually Papa, Pavel Shavlovsky, who stands over the stove while his wife and daughter tend to the surprisingly diverse cast of customers—Russian émigrés, retirees, and construction workers—who rub elbows at the counter running the length of the narrow room. This is a serious bare-bones, no-thrills breakfast joint with one booth at the back and a few tables; the best seats are at the counter, where the full force of sizzling bacon and the crack of another egg on the griddle will send an  appetite spiraling out of control. Though there are not a lot of options, what they do here they do well. The hash browns are made from fresh potatoes, the toast from homemade bread; both accompany the generous omelets and combination egg plates. For lunch there's more along the lines of classic diner food, and almost everything touches the griddle—burgers, patty melts, Reuben sandwiches. In fact, if it weren't for the Russian accents and the borscht, this place couldn't be any more American. *Breakfast, lunch Mon–Sat; no credit cards; no checks; no alcohol.*

MANILA'S BEST

4811 SE Powell Blvd
☎ *(503) 788-6454*
SE Powell *Filipino*

For years Portland had been so well stocked in restaurants representing cuisines across the globe, it might have escaped attention that there was no Filipino food until Manila's Best opened in 1997. Now there's a reason, beyond videos and fast food, to visit this particularly benighted stretch of SE Powell Boulevard: exotic flavors—a mix of Spanish and Asian, as you might imagine from the Philippines' colonial history. Pork and shrimp dishes abound; your server may gently remind you that some of the shrimp dishes are cooked in a shrimp stock, imparting a strong flavor. This is heaven to Filipinos and others familiar with the tastes of Southeast Asia, and ultimately it should be no problem for Anglo tastebuds that enjoy flavors from the sea. Some dishes are served with rice, some with noodles, but all are saucy, spicy, and bring a new twist to combinations you might be used to from Thai or Vietnamese food. Don't be surprised by the children who run between the kitchen and sparse, brightly lit dining room in this family-owned and run establishment. If you're lucky, the elderly gentleman friend of the family will stop in the night you're here to play the accordion and do magic tricks. *Lunch, dinner Tues–Sat; AE, DIS, MC, V; checks OK; no alcohol.*

MARCO'S CAFE AND ESPRESSO BAR
7910 SW 35th Ave
☎ *(503) 245-0199*
Multnomah   🍴 *Inventive Ethnic*

In the stroller's paradise of antique-rich Multnomah, Marco's has near-landmark status. The sunny dining rooms have high ceilings and intriguing prints on the walls, and there's a rack of reading material by the front door. It's lovely anytime—but some prefer breakfast because of options like the French toast stuffed with apples and cinnamon and drenched with apple-flavored syrup, while others swear by the variety of organic burgers at lunch or the delicious main-course salads large enough to share. Then there are the southwest Portlanders who prefer to wait for evenings, when Marco's turns into an imaginative dinner operation, with nightly changing entrees such as spanokopita and Chicken Roma, as well as pastas and a good variety of vegetarian dishes. The desserts are Marco's own and never fail to satisfy a sweet tooth. Children fit right in. *Breakfast, lunch every day, dinner Mon–Sat; AE, DC, DIS, MC, V; local checks only; beer and wine.* &

MARINEPOLIS
4021 SW 117th Ave (Canyonplace Shopping Center), Beaverton
☎ *(503) 520-0257*
Beaverton   🍴 *Japanese*

Teaching your kids about sushi can be like teaching them about caviar: for your wallet's sake, you almost hope they don't like it. But in this branch of a Japanese chain (that somehow landed in a Beaverton shopping mall), the instruction can be relatively painless, and even entertaining. Decent, inexpensive sushi circles around the dining area on a conveyor belt; you pick off what you want, and when you're finished the waitress counts the plates. Kids are

enthralled, the fish is fine, and even if there's a certain assembly-line feel to it, the kitchen does take requests. And you don't even have to teach your kid to say *maguro*—just have them point and pick. *Lunch, dinner every day; MC, V; no checks; beer, wine, and sake.* ♿

MARSEE BAKING

935 NE Broadway (and branches)
☎ *(503) 280-8800*
NE Broadway-Lloyd Center/Downtown/Lake
Oswego/Northwest/Portland Airport/Westmoreland   ✕ *Bakery*

Unless you take your mother to Marsee Baking, no one will care if you have dessert instead of lunch. With its shiny pastry case packed with goodies, Marsee is a great place to indulge sweet cravings. Like with

the Chocolate Crinkle Cookie—crisp on the outside and densely fudgy on the inside; it's not just a cookie, it's an *experience*—for a mere 90 cents. However, if you insist on paring nutrients with your calories, there is a "build-your-own" sandwich menu: choose from a selection of Marsee's excellent fresh breads and fill with your choice of meats, cheeses, veggies, and spreads. There are

also several winning sandwich combinations served on Marsee's bagels, as well as soups, pizzalike foccacia, and prepackaged salads. Be forewarned: counter service can be confused and confusing; be sure to grab a numbered ticket before standing in line. Recent expansion has put branches throughout the Portland metro area and into Washington State, and has staked an outpost at the Portland International Airport—an instant antidote to airplane food. *Breakfast, lunch, dinner every day; DIS, MC, V; local checks only; no alcohol.* ♿

MCCORMICK AND SCHMICK'S

235 SW First Ave (and branch)
☎ *(503) 224-7522*
Downtown/Beaverton   ✕ *Happy Hour*

For fans of beautiful bars, McCormick and Schmick's satisfies before the first bite. Although the bar was built along with the restaurant in 1979, it glows with a patina more ancient than its years. Slacking hipster bartenders have no place here; instead, competent restaurant professionals whose experience renders them close to psychic run the show. Even the best bars tend to have quiet times, and that's where special promotions (a.k.a. happy hour) come to play. The happy hour menu here is generous in several ways: menu variety, portion size, and the hours during which it's available—1:30pm to 6:30pm and 9:30pm to close Monday through

Friday, 4:30pm to 6:30pm and 9:30pm to close on Saturday, and from 4:30pm to close on Sunday (the Beaverton branch, 9945 SW Beaverton-Hillsdale Highway, 503/643-1322; offers slightly different hours, call before you go). There are a dozen dishes, each priced at $1.95, and one or two of them make an ample meal. The Tillamook Cheddar Burger and Wild Mushroom Ravioli are the two most popular menu items, and rightfully so: the first pairs eight ounces of beef, cooked to order, with tomato, red onion, lettuce, pickles and fries. This is no silver-dollar-dinky-burger scam in which you end up ordering five items to make a meal; in every way, including price, this burger puts the Golden Arches to shame. The ravioli arrive plump and shi-itake-scented in a warm bath of cheesy sauce. Other bar menu items include sautéed mushroom caps, baked polenta with creole sauce, and chicken wings with garlic sauce. On top of great food bargains, McCormick and Schmick's has a healthy selection of beer, wine, and mixed drinks, along with an extensive Scotch list. *Happy hour every day; AE, DC, DIS, JCB, MC, V; no checks; full bar.* ♿

MCMENAMIN'S KENNEDY SCHOOL

5736 NE 33rd Ave
☎ *(503) 249-3983*
Northeast, Beyond 39th ✗ *Pub Grub*

Portland's McMenamin brothers have done it again: taken the most unlikely and neglected building and funkily restored it into a multi-use fun house that includes a restaurant, two bars, a theater, public meeting rooms, hotel rooms, and a swimming pool. In this case the building was once an elementary school; now the classrooms accommodate overnight guests. As for the restaurant, it's a far cry from cafeteria food. Located along the interior courtyard (which, when weather permits, makes a delightful place for drinking one of the famous McMenamin microbrews), the kitchen offers a full line of adolescent-pleasing, hippy-themed pub food heavy on burgers, fries, and pizza. With a nod to the boomer clientele, there are also items such as the hummus platter, a three-cheese quesadilla, and warm Brie with roasted garlic and kalamata olives. Specialties of the house range from a steak sandwich zipped with chipotle mayo and sweetened with caramelized onions, to rich portobello ravioli in a roasted garlic basil cream sauce. Sometimes on busy nights the pizza kitchen and the burger kitchen have trouble coordinating orders, but if your table is lucky, all heads will be down at the same time while you do your homework on the large plates. Lots of singles, families, and civic groups keep the Kennedy School's long hallways busy well into the evenings. Hotel guests and Sunday brunchers choose from a variety of standard omelets, biscuits and gravy, chicken-fried steak, granola, and bagels. Malt O' Meal is also a special trip down memory lane, as is the Detention Room bar for smokers. *Lunch, dinner every day; AE, DIS, MC, V; checks OK; full bar.* &

MI RANCHITO TAQUERIA
2839 NE Alberta St
☎ *(503) 331-1774*
Alberta St   ✗ Mexican

Along with its next-door neighbor, La Sirenita, Mi Ranchito Taqueria vies for the Alberta Street lunch crowd with fresh and authentic burritos, tacos, tamales, and quesadillas. Mi Ranchito, though, feels more like a family diner, opening at 9am for breakfasts of *chorizo* and eggs and huevos rancheros (among others—all $3.75), and the proverbial bottomless cup of coffee. Servings are generous. Under the watchful eyes of Our Lady of Guadalupe, roomy booths accommodate parties of four or more and invite lingering with the newspaper or with friends. The pace seems slower here—much care is taken with the preparation and presentation of the food. Accompaniments of fresh salsas, pickled vegetables, and Mexican music round out the extensive lunch and dinner selections—not mere taqueria food, but full restaurant fare. The soups (including *menudo* and *pozole*) make meals in themselves. Burritos are enormous—come famished if you expect to finish one. Combination meals, at $5.50 for lunch or dinner, include rice, beans, and tortillas; they're very good. The *enchiladas verdes de queso con pollo* (cheese and chicken enchiladas with green chile) will make a believer out of anyone. A wide variety of juices and soft drinks is available, but—sorry—no alcohol. *Breakfast, lunch, dinner every day; no credit cards; no checks; no alcohol.* &

MIO SUSHI
2271 NW Johnson St
☎ *(503) 221-1469*
Northwest   ✗ *Japanese*

As its name suggests, sushi is where Mio Sushi shines: the sushi case swims with glistening fish that show up on the plate fresh and pretty. But there are other things, like sushi shrimp *"pizza"*—rice, seaweed, and fish or shrimp baked then topped with a special sauce and green onions—as well as soothing, inexpensive ramen and udon soups. For a cheap date, order (judiciously) a few sushi rolls, or try one of the bento entrees, which come with soup, salad, and rice. Other unusual menu items are advertised on charming handwritten signs hung on the walls of this small but cozy, bare-bones sushi den. Though unassuming, come weekends this place can fill up. *Lunch, dinner Mon–Sat; AE, MC, V; no checks; beer and wine.*

MISOHAPI
1123 NW 23rd Ave
☎ *(503) 796-2012*
Northwest   ✗ *Thai/Vietnamese*

If you're craving comfort noodle dishes—charcoal chicken with vermicelli (a winner), phad thai (nice, too), or flavor-rich yakisoba with skewered teriyaki chicken—and you're in northwest Portland, this is the place to go. Some of the less starchy Thai or Vietnamese entrees like the ginger beef, black bean garlic pork, or the self-proclaimed Thai-style General Tso's chicken (we were convinced) are also quite good. Misohapi does a brisk lunch business, offering either bento boxes to go (skewered meat over rice with a tasty cabbage salad) or the lunch special: soup or salad plus an entree chosen from a list of 25 possibilities. The new space, just a couple blocks north from the original, is a bit more sleek than the last, drawing the scrub set from Good Samaritan Hospital, as well as business types looking for a quick lunch between meetings. On nice days you can take your meal outside to a  table on NW 23rd Avenue, and watch passersby rubberneck your meal. *Lunch, dinner Mon–Sat; DIS, MC, V; local checks only; beer and wine.* ♿

MONTE CARLO RESTAURANT

1016 SE Belmont St
☎ *(503) 238-7627*
Southest, Close In   ✗ *Italian*

Portland's oldest (since 1927) Italian restaurant is a dining institution rediscovered and reclaimed by each new generation; a survey of the crowd on any given night will attest to its popularity. Unswayed by the

vagaries of culinary fashion, the Monte Carlo uncompromisingly dishes out authentic Italian-American food, and lots of it. Red walls and carpet, cushy booths along the wall, and vaguely baroque paintings over-head serve as backdrop to the hearty food like spaghetti and meatballs. Good, old-fash-ioned garlic bread is the perfect vehicle for mopping up every last bit of sauce. The wine list is small but eclectic, and a large carafe of house wine can be had for practically the same price as a single glass at other restaurants. If you're not completely exhausted after all this carbo-loading, head up to the adjacent lounge for a little more kitsch: cocktails and a spin on the dance floor; on Sundays there's live R&B. *Lunch Mon−Fri, dinner every day; AE, DC, DIS, M, V; checks OK; full bar.* ♿

MORNING STAR ESPRESSO

510 SW 3rd Ave
☎ *(503) 241-2401*
Downtown   ✗ *Coffeehouse*

Framed "Morning Star News" posters line the walls of this warm cof-feehouse with headlines, making larger-than-life claims like "Elvis Is in My Coffee Cup" and "Woman Gives Birth to Double Latte." Other humorous notes show up in decorating touches—like the squashed Peeps under the glass table tops—and the attitude of the staff. Morn-ings here bring in a parade of people—advertising hipsters, student types, slackers, and suits—for pastries, bagels, and coffee. Lunch draws the same demographics for its excellent sandwiches: a good 20 or so flavors, all served on Grand Central bread with a handful of Tim's Cascade chips and orange slices. With a glass of milk, Mom would be proud. (Although she might wonder at the sign on the counter: "Please, if you're a junkie, don't ask for the bathroom key, unless you purchase a sandwich. Thank you.") *Breakfast, lunch Mon−Sat; no credit cards; checks OK; no alcohol.* ♿

NANCY LEE'S PHARMACY FOUNTAIN

2334 W Burnside St
☎ (503) 241-1137
West Hills   ✕ American

You're not only walking into an inviting breakfast and lunch place,
you're also walking into 1955. This old soda fountain inside the Town
Pharmacy is what nostalgia should be, but hardly ever is: the waitresses smile, the omelets fluff, and every other Thursday there are
hand-carved turkey sandwiches. Almost all the
swiveling bar stools in the long, narrow eatery are
occupied by folks who know the waitresses by name
and who order eggs and hashbrowns for breakfast,
half a grilled meat loaf sandwich and a cup of
tomato soup for lunch, and maybe share a late-
afternoon milk shake. Don't even think of asking for
an espresso. *Breakfast, lunch Mon–Sat; no credit
cards; local checks only; no alcohol.*

NATURE'S MARKETPLACE

8024 E Mill Plain Blvd, Vancouver, WA (and branches)
☎ (360) 695-8878
Vancouver, WA and Vicinity/Beaverton/Fremont/Hillsdale/
Lake Oswego/Laurelhurst/SE Division   ✕ Deli

Nature's, Portland's longtime-favorite natural foods store, arrived in
Vancouver a couple years ago, updating the food scene in southwest
Washington with its wide selection of organic produce and hormone-
free meat, cooking classes, ready-to-cook foods, and a grocer's restaurant that's good enough to grab some headlines. Take out or eat your
food here in the bright and ecologically correct Cafe Court. You'll find
ethnic dips, casseroles, salads, pizzas, tasty spuds at the baked potato
bar, marinated meats, European breads, rich desserts, and even breakfast. The most recent addition to what's becoming a natural foods
empire is the state of the art Boones Ferry store (503/635-8950); at
other more modest outlets there's great takeout to be had in the way
of sandwiches, burritos, soups, and salads. *Open every day; DIS, MC,
V; checks OK; beer and wine.*

NICHOLAS' RESTAURANT

318 SE Grand Ave
☎ (503) 235-5123
Southeast, Close In   ✕ Middle Eastern

It would be easy to drive by this place and never know what lies behind
the red door of the nondescript storefront. If you do, you're missing
out on one of the great food finds in Portland. People in the know—
from suits to students—gather in this simple, small restaurant to feast
on delicious, inexpensive Middle Eastern and Greek food. Try anything
here—from creamy, garlicky tzatziki to the unusual and enticing
Mediterranean pizza, made exotic by the extraordinary toppings and
spices. The falafel is arguably the best in town and the hummus unbe-
lievably creamy. The only thing lacking (besides the undeniably divey
decor) is the choice of beverages: soda pop, a weird yogurt drink, and
weak Turkish coffee. *Lunch, dinner every day; no credit cards; checks
OK; no alcohol.*

NOAH'S NEW YORK BAGELS

500 NW 23rd Ave (and branches)
☎ (503) 222-7995
Northwest/Beaverton/Hawthorne/Hillsdale/Lake Oswego   ✕ Bagels

Noah's New York Bagels, with its black-and-white photos of The City
and Dodgers banners tacked on the walls, begs you to believe that
their bagel shops will transport you to Brooklyn without the airfare.
But let's face it: Noah's is headquartered in Alameda, California, and
makes sacrilegiously flavored bagels such as banana nut and chocolate chip—oy vey! Since this is not New York, exceptions can be made;
as far as bagels go in Portland, these are some of the best. And, with
five shops in the Portland metro area, buying bagels and Jewish delicatessen food means not having to travel too far outside your neighborhood. Bagel sandwiches, taller than the average mouth and
nonetheless appealing for it, make a nice change for lunch. Pile on the
smoked whitefish salad, lox and
cream cheese, hummus, or flavored cream cheese—schmeers
as they're called here—or go
with meatier choices like corned
beef, turkey, or pastrami-style
turkey.  Sandwiches come with the usual condiments and a pickle half.
Noah's will also pack bagels to go and breakfast platters to feed a
crowd, in addition to brown bagging their sandwiches, salads, and, in

the nonkosher store, soups. Until a few years ago Noah's stores kept kosher; now all but the Hillsdale store have phased out their kosher kitchens. The bottom line is that what Noah's lacks in authenticity and homegrown flavor, it makes up for in reliability and convenience. *Breakfast, lunch Mon–Sun; AE (pending), MC, V; checks OK; no alcohol.* ♿

NOB HILL BAR & GRILL
937 NW 23rd Ave
☎ *(503) 274-9616*
Northwest   🍴 *Pub Grub*

Known simply as the Nobby, this corner spot is the last vestige of the kind of local tavern that once flourished in this Northwest neighborhood. A haven for longtime residents as well as anyone looking to escape the gauntlet of gentrification, the Nobby is a spirited, lively meeting place. With three competing television sets—one directly on the bar—a pool table, and video poker, there are plenty of distractions, but your best bet is to nab a window seat for people watching, both inside and out. Regulars (including an ex-mayor) converge at the bar beneath a giant display of beer steins. A broad beer selection, heavy on local micros, is reason alone to come, but those in the know stop in for one of the better tavern burgers in town, as well as nightly specials: 50-cent tacos on Monday and steak specials the rest of the week after 5pm. For $7.95, it's your choice of a 7- to 8-ounce filet, New York, or rib-eye steak with fries, baked potato, or potato salad, plus soup or salad with garlic toast. *Breakfast, lunch, dinner every day; DIS, MC, V; no checks; beer and wine.*

NOHO'S HAWAIIAN CAFE
2525 SE Clinton St (and branch)
☎ *(503) 233-5301*
Clinton St/SW Macadam Ave-Johns Landing   🍴 *Hawaiian*

This is a place to put away some serious food. Korean-cut short ribs, marinated in honey, garlic, and sesame seed sauce, are sublime; Phil's Ono Chicken is infused in a ginger sauce and cooked until the bird is as tender as tuna. Matter of fact, ahi is available too, as is pork—sometimes as a special. Dinners are available in three sizes that translate—in our minds, at least—to medium, large, or mega-portions, and come with rice and a macaroni or green salad. There's also a yakisoba noodle plate

with four choices of sauce. Noho's (formerly Local Boyz) is usually packed; if you can't get a table to put that food away on the premises, you might consider taking it home. Or, check out the new location near Johns Landing (0515 SW Carolina Street, 503/977-2771), where the more upscale setting draws—you got it—a more upscale crowd. *Lunch, dinner every day; AE, MC, V; checks OK; no alcohol.* &

NONNA EMILIA RISTORANTE ITALIANO

17210 SW Shaw St, Aloha
☎ *(503) 649-2232*
Beaverton *Italian*

Nonna Emilia must have been the kind of Italian grandmother who always had something delicious cooking on the stove. Grandson Stephen Ceccanti honors his "nonna" with a restaurant that feels like a family reunion. Photos of Emilia and the Ceccantis grace the walls, and the aroma of handed-down recipes fills the air. This is a popular family spot; expect a wait on Fridays and Saturdays, when no reservations are taken. The menu consists of the usual Italian fare, including spaghetti and lasagne, plus some surprises such as Calamari Parmigiana and Veal Scaloppine alla Emilia. The meat sauce, Nonna's own recipe made with 11 herbs and spices, is  rich and hearty. The thick-crust pizzas are a treat that even a vegan can enjoy—they offer vegetarian toppings and soy cheese on a whole wheat crust. Specialties and pasta dishes range from $7.95 to $14.95, while pizzas start at $9.95. Service is prompt, and the intimate and elegant atmosphere is enhanced by subdued lighting and crisp table linens. Besides spumoni ice cream, Emilia offers New York–style cheesecake and peanut butter pie for dessert. Not exactly Italian, but just what you might expect your grandmother to tempt you with after an already filling meal. *Lunch Tues–Fri, dinner every day; AE, DC, DIS, MC, V; local checks OK; full bar.* &

OASIS CAFE

3701 SE Hawthorne Blvd
☎ *(503) 231-0901*
Hawthorne *Pizza*

This feel-good corner cafe at the intersection of Hawthorne Boulevard and 37th Street brings together the two factions of the neighborhood—

hip student types and post-hippie closet yuppies who'd rather you didn't know they own a house just around the corner. Ownership is not what it's all about, though—seizing the moment is. And no moment is better than the one when you take your first bite of Oasis pizza—chewy crust, spicy sauce, stringy cheese, hot pepperoni. In addition to the several pies by the slice, there are a number of whole pie options, from classics like Canadian bacon and pineapple, to totally vernacular concoctions like Mr. Toad's Wild Ride (a popular veggie pizza with mushrooms, artichoke hearts, fresh tomatoes, and onions). If coming

up with your own wild ride is more your style, there are a million choices to make, starting with the base coat (pesto, tomato, or white cream sauce), moving through the cheese layer (mozzarella, Gorgonzola, feta, and/or cheddar), and making your way to the final standard and not-so-standard (jalapeños, cilantro, avocado) toppings. Also on the menu: calzones, hot sandwiches, and lots of salads, from your basic dinner salad with sliced black olives and blue cheese dressing, to larger, full-meal offerings (Greek, spinach, taco). A few good beers on tap (Pilsner Urquell, Widmer) and the espresso machine guarantee that there's always someone hanging out here, whether it's mealtime or not. *Lunch, dinner every day; DIS, MC, V; checks OK; beer and wine.* &

OLD SPAGHETTI FACTORY

0715 SW Bancroft St
☎ *(503) 222-5375*
SW Macadam Ave-Johns Landing   ✕ *Italian*

In an immense building on the west bank of the Willamette sits the international headquarters for this chain of more than two dozen restaurants that began in Portland. It's the place to join 35 of your closest friends for a spaghetti dinner—just don't set your expectations for the food too high. Dinners include an iceberg lettuce salad (which is about as good as it could be), chewy sourdough bread, and spumoni ice cream. You might try the Manager's Favorite Spaghetti (any two sauces), with marinara on one half and browned butter and mizithra cheese on the other. An amazing assemblage of antiques—and a restored trolley car—provide lots of distraction throughout the several dining areas, and it's worth going upstairs to step on the magnificent old brass scale. Reservations are not accepted, and there's often a wait, but you can stroll along the river or hang out upstairs in the bar while doing so; when your table is ready, your name will be blasted over the sound system. *Lunch, dinner every day; AE, DC, DIS, MC, V; checks OK; full bar.* ♿

OLD WIVES' TALES

1300 E Burnside St
☎ *(503) 238-0470*
Southeast, Close In   🍴 *Inventive Ethnic*

Come here with the kids. What with the playroom and the turkey franks, it's a healthful alternative to the ball pit and burgers at McDonald's. Even without a shorty in tow, it's a good place to meet for lunch—just ask for a table far away from the one in which half of the eight seats are high chairs. When Holly Hart opened the restaurant in the early '80s, it doubled as a feminist gathering place, with a back room where men and women met for heated discussions, and an indestructible playroom for the younger set.

Now, although the playroom is still an important part of the ambiance, the back room has long since become the "quiet room." The food and mood are the same as they were in the early days, and although intriguingly adult things are done to seafood, the motif continues to be whole-wheat correctness. On the menu you'll find Hungarian mushroom soup (something like a meatless

stroganoff), vegetarian enchiladas, and carrot-cashew burgers, plus hot pastrami sandwiches or a chicken-topped caesar for the unconverted. The children's menu meets parental approval—but kids will like it too. *Breakfast, lunch, dinner every day; AE, DIS, MC, V; checks OK; beer and wine.* ♿

THE ORIGINAL PANCAKE HOUSE

8600 SW Barbur Blvd
☎ *(503) 246-9007*
Burlingame   🍴 *American*

Lots of things may have changed in Portland, but the people waiting patiently outside this landmark restaurant seem to have been there since 1953. This place hums from the time it opens at 7am practically until it closes in midafternoon. The sourdough flapjacks—from wine-spiked cherry to wheat germ to a behemoth apple pancake with a sticky cinnamon glaze—are made from scratch. A good bet is the egg-rich Dutch baby, which arrives looking like a huge, sunken birthday cake, dusted with powdered sugar and served with fresh lemon. Omelets big enough for two (made from a half-dozen eggs) arrive with a short stack. The service is cheerful and efficient; after all, there are people waiting for your table. *Breakfast, lunch Wed–Sun; no credit cards; checks OK; no alcohol.*

PASTA BELLA

709 SW 17th Ave
☎ *(503) 248-4614*
Downtown *Italian*

Located on the new westbound MAX line, Pasta Bella broadens the downtown lunch circle and makes a good stop for dinner on the way home. Undeniably modern in its shape and form, efforts to make the interior cozy include framed posters, pottery bowls and plates along the walls, and fresh flowers at each table. Pasta Bella isn't trying to reinvent the wheel when it comes to pasta, but if you're looking for a heaping bowl of noodles with a good basic sauce, you can't go wrong here. Choices include spaghetti with marinara, linguini Bolognese, roasted walnut and garlic ravioli with  a cream sauce, and Seafood Calbrera (clams, mussels, and shrimp on top of linguini). Dishes like chicken primavera or papparadelle with pork feature fresh poultry and meat from Ladd's Meats. Also worth noting: salads and a selection of wines by the glass from the wine bar. *Lunch, dinner Tues–Sat; MC, V; checks OK; beer and wine.* ♿

PASTA VELOCE

1022 SW Morrison St
☎ *(503) 916-4388*
Downtown *Italian*

In its short life, Pasta Veloce has rocketed to the top of many a down-towner's list of favorite places to grab lunch, and it's easy to see why: here is where Italian comfort fare and fast food meet, a place where you can loosen your tie, fill your belly—and be back at your desk in an hour. When the owners of NE Broadway's neighborhood Italian restaurant Rustica decided to go after the noon crowd, they opened the airy two-tier Pasta Veloce on the MAX line at SW Morrison Street, between 10th and 11th Avenues. Since 1997, Pasta Veloce has been feeding hungry clerks and business people a steady diet of interesting pastas—like penne with spinach, butternut squash, cream, and Parmesan. You order at the counter, then find a seat at one of the simple blonde tables downstairs or up—or take your boxed meal back to the lunchroom. It's satisfying fare that's not bad for you (unlike much fast food), and you can count on the wait being short. But a cheap eat? You'll see: a plate of pasta with a slice of hearty grilled bread alongside will cost around $5; add a green salad for another $1.95. And the red wine, itself a bargain at $3 a glass, is generously poured. Panini, too. *Lunch, dinner Mon—Sat; MC, V; checks OK; beer and wine.* &

PAZZORIA BAKERY AND CAFE

621 SW Washington St
☎ *(503) 228-1695*
Downtown   ✗ Italian

A simple menu serves this swanky downtown cafe well. A freshly made soup of the day, several panini, and a selection of salads are all Pazzoria needs to offer. The panini are delicious—smoked turkey with talegio cheese and honey mustard on a seeded roll; prosciutto cotto with fresh mozzarella, tomato, and Dijon mustard on foccacia; and warm grilled eggplant, roasted peppers, goat cheese and lemon vinaigrette. Soups vary from tomato bisque to minestrone and come by the cup or bowl. Salads options include mixed greens, pasta with Parmesan, arugula with fennel or roasted potatoes with grain mustard, and sweet peppers and parsley. A choice of three salads with bread goes for $4.50. In addition to these constants, there is often a pizza and usually a daily chalkboard special. Lines may be out the door, but the hardworking servers are efficient, friendly, and conscientious. The atmosphere imitates that of an upscale Italian cafe—European posters, glassware, and artisan breads. In the late afternoon, it's a quiet place to read the paper with a cappuccino, or drop in after work before going out for a generous plate of antipasti and a glass of wine. *Break-fast, lunch Mon—Sat; AE, DC, MC, V; no checks; beer and wine.* &

PEARL BAKERY

102 NW 9th Ave
☎ *(503) 827-0910*
Pearl District
✗ *Bakery*

From the irresistible pastries and incredible breads to the light-filled room and pretty blue bags, everything about the Pearl is done with great taste. The artisan breads—pain poolish, levain, and ciabatta—are leavened by traditional methods, hand formed, and baked in the huge ovens in the back; people who work in the neighborhood set their watches to the time their favorite loaves come out of the oven. Others stop in for coffee and pastries—perhaps the chocolate panini or a lemon danish—or one of the delicious sandwiches (eggplant on ciabatta, pears and Gorgonzola on walnut levain, smoked turkey on a Kaiser roll) from the case. Consider yourself forewarned: a visit to the bakery in the afternoon means limited choices; if there's something you absolutely must have, go early. *Breakfast, lunch Mon–Sat; no credit cards; checks OK; no alcohol.* ♿

PERRY'S ON FREMONT

2401 NE Fremont St
☎ *(503) 287-3655*
Alameda-Beaumont
 American

The first thing you see on entering Perry's are the huge—and hugely popular—pies; this place moves a lot of marionberry. Then your eyes move to the great tic-tac-toe brownies and huge slabs of cake. Perry's draws lots of kids (and their parents) with its cheeseburgers and milk shakes; it's virtually the Alameda-Beaumont neighborhood's family center. Those dining with tykes appreciate the varied menu, which features a chicken pot pie that's everything chicken pot pie is supposed to be, and catfish burgers. When weather allows the courtyard is a fine place to cool off with lemonade or ice cream. *Lunch on Saturday only, dinner Tues–Sat; AE, DC, DIS, MC, V; checks OK; full bar.* ♿

PERSIAN HOUSE RESTAURANT

1026 SW Morrison St
☎ *(503) 243-1430*
Downtown   ✕ *Middle Eastern*

Negotiating polite downtown Portland is rarely enervating, but should you feel a need to duck the hustle and bustle, take refuge at Persian House on Morrison Street, downtown's unofficial restaurant row. Here is the perfect place to eat lunch alone, a cozy nest with all the comforts a single diner requires—a quiet room, a $5.99 lunch buffet, unobtrusive waitresses, and a big, sloppy stock of pop culture magazines. That said, the food is best at night when you bring friends and order lots of different things from the mostly Iranian dinner menu. The appetizers are excellent and meant for sharing. Try the sweet and sour eggplant, a silken revelation with pomegranate glaze, mint, and garlic, or the tangy and savory spinach yogurt dip. The food here feels bright, and there is a refreshing variety of vegetarian dishes for the Gardenburger-weary: spinach and prune *koresh*, or stew; vegetarian paella; and yellow split peas with dry lime. Carnivores should order the succulent, falling-off-the-bone lamb shank, delicately spiced and served with dilled rice. Rice, the staple of Iran, is well made here, each kernel fragrant and separate. Dinner entrees include soup or salad bar, and a cup of aromatic Persian tea completes the experience. *Lunch, dinner Mon–Sat; AE, DC, DIS, MC, V; no checks; beer and wine.* &

PHIL'S UPTOWN MEAT MARKET

17 NW 23rd Pl
☎ *(503) 224-9541*
Northwest   ✕ *Bento*

Everyone with a grill and a pot serves "bento" these days—or at least the grilled skewers of meat called bento. While a butcher shop may seem an unlikely locale for a ready-made meal, smack-dab in front of Phil's Uptown Market you'll find one of the best little operations around. From late morning through afternoon, smoke spews from the grill while stick after stick of the plumpest, tastiest white-meat chicken is plopped onto massive beds of rice and doused with teriyaki and sweet-hot sauce before being handed to the next patient person in line. Some take their lunch home or back to the office, others polish off their meal on the steps or in the front seat of their car. *Lunch Mon–Sat; MC, V; checks OK; wine sold by the bottle inside.*

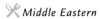

PHO HUNG

4717 SE Powell Blvd (and branches)
☎ *(503) 775-3170*
SE Powell/Beaverton/Northeast, Beyond 39th ✖ *Vietnamese*

This is one of Portland's busiest beef noodle houses, its dining room a swirl of hungry families, rushing waiters, and steamy aromas of Vietnam's national dish—*pho*. For less than $5 you can immerse yourself in a curative bowl—"tureen" might be more accurate—of sublime beef broth loaded with rice noodles, slivers of beef, and fresh herbs. Soups are served with a garnish plate of bean sprouts, basil, jalapeño, and lime wedges to sweeten or sour an already sinus-clearing experience; an assortment of Asian hot sauces and *nuoc mam* (fermented fish sauce) boost the megatonnage. Order with your brain and not your stomach; many people never even finish the small, which rings in at a mere $3.75. Though Portland foodies praise Pho Hung's beef broth, the chicken noodle soup is even better: a sweet and soothing broth with tangles of slippery noodles, scallions, and tender slices of chicken that actually taste like chicken. Finish your meal with Vietnamese hot or iced coffee (brewed to order and served with sweetened condensed milk), gratifyingly strong and tasty. In Vietnam they eat *pho* for breakfast, and here you can eat it morning, noon, and night. *Breakfast, lunch, dinner every day; AE, DC, DIS, JCB, MC, V; checks OK; no alcohol.* ♿

PHO VAN

1919 SE 82nd Ave
☎ *(503) 788-5244*
Southeast, Beyond 39th ✖ *Vietnamese*

In the range of cheap eats, where at one end it requires a strategy to stay within a $30 budget, and at the other you feast like kings and queens, Pho Van treats you like royalty. What was once a dive with great *pho* is now a lovely restaurant with great *pho*. You're surrounded by slate floors, high ceilings, wood booths, and windows—amidst such a stylish decor it's hard to believe that the most expensive thing on the menu rings in at $7.50. Let the feast begin with fresh salad rolls and crispy rice-flour crêpes. Follow it with a bowl of *pho*, the heart-warming Vietnamese noodle soup that combines a wonderfully flavored meat broth with rice noodles, your choice of meat (round steak, shredded tripe, meatballs, lean brisket), and a heap of fresh flavors and textures to add to your liking—basil or mint leaves, chiles, lime, bean sprouts. Though it's easy to always order *pho* (even the small bowls are large here), the grilled entrees, like the lemongrass-marinated chicken on rice with a side of delicious pickled cabbage with carrots and daikon radish, are also very good. To wash it all down there's a bevy of exotic beverages—sour sop and jackfruit smoothies, fresh lime juice, coffee with condensed milk—as well as local and Asian beers. The proprietors' latest enterprise is a new noodle shop, Mi Van, at the old location down the street (707 NE 82nd Avenue; 503/254-0258). *Lunch, dinner every day; DIS, MC, V; no checks; beer only.* ♿

THE PIED COW
3244 SE Belmont St
☎ *(503) 230-4866*
Belmont   ✗ *Coffeehouse*

This is where Jeannie—as in *I Dream of Jeannie*—would hang now if she were into '70s self-parody; the front room of this colorful Victorian bears a strong resemblance to her bottle, with its bay window dressed in beads, lace curtains, and low couches with pillows covered in leopard-print fabric. Neo-hippies, retro-bohemians, and bookish types of all ages come here to read the *New York Times*, play cards, and ponder over a cup of coffee—is it half full or half empty? This is the ultimate coffeehouse: the food—various plates of bread and cheese, hummus and smoked salmon, as well as soups and salads—is cheap, the cappuccinos are delicious, and there's always a satisfyingly rich chocolate dessert. Add to that an excellent tea list (try the Redwood Chai) and a delightful courtyard lit by candles and lanterns, and there's no better place to while away a warm summer evening. *Dinner Tues–Fri; lunch, dinner Sat–Sun; no credit cards; no checks; beer and wine.*

PIZZA LUNA
1708 NE Broadway (and branch)
☎ *(503) 335-3059*
NE Broadway-Lloyd Center/Cedar Hills   ✗ *Pizza*

Pizza here is represented in more phases than luna herself: by the slice, from one of six daily pies, or in whole pies, from the list of 25

established combinations. Thin
crusts and Italian ingredients
come together to make a heavenly pizza, like the sublime Carbonara, topped with a pepper
bacon infused bechamel sauce,
caramelized onions, and mush-

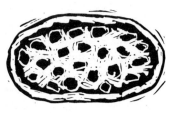

rooms. The zesty Portofino starts with a base of olive oil, fresh garlic,
and basil, to which roasted garlic, peppers, chèvre, and sun-dried
tomatoes are added. Pizza carnivores won't be disappointed by Luna's
11 choices of meat toppings, which include Cariani pepperoni, Italian
sausage, and prosciutto; you won't find any of those overwhelmingly
salted, thick plastic circles that often land on other pizzas. Other menu
items worth noting include a superb spinach salad with lots of fresh
leafy dark greens, thinly sliced onions, crumbled feta, and salty kalamata olives; huge calzones; meatball or eggplant sandwiches; spinach-
mushroom cannelloni; and vegetarian or seafood lasagne. Though the
pizza and the trompe l'oeil mural allude to a calm Italian piazza, the
view out the window is pure Portland. There's another location in
Cedar Hills: 7535 SW Barnes Road, (503) 292-3500. *Lunch, dinner
every day; MC, V; checks OK; beer and wine.* &

PIZZICATO
705 SW Alder St (and branches)
☎ *(503) 226-1007*
Downtown/Gresham/Hillsdale/Laurelhurst/Northwest/
Oak Hills/West Hills/West Linn/Westmoreland   *Pizza*

These yupscale gourmet pizzerias tower over their megachain competitors and over many local pizza places that have been in business a lot
longer. Credit Pizzicato's success to the imaginative pairings of fresh
ingredients on pies (red potatoes and prosciutto, for instance), as well
as classics—like pepperoni—done with respect. There's a caesar salad
that's garlicky good, and a daily special, which you can buy by the slice
for lunch at most locations. The best bet may be the simplest: the luscious pizza Margherita is little more than crust, tomatoes, and cheese,
but it's divine. Though the theme and the menu are pretty much the
same everywhere, each branch offers a little something different in the
way of ambiance; the downtown shop courts a brisk lunch crowd with
the added attraction of foccacia sandwiches. *Lunch, dinner every day;
AE, MC, V; checks OK; beer and wine.* &

PORTLAND BREWHOUSE TAPROOM AND GRILL

2730 NW 31st Ave
☎ (503) 228-5269
Northwest   ✗ Pub Grub

There's nothing "micro" about this microbrewer's showpiece brewpub in northwest Portland's industrial zone. Behind the huge copper kettles at the entrance, there's plenty of space for diners to pull up a seat, either in the main room; the smaller, quieter back room; or on the inviting patio outside. Beer is the thing here, and the food is a good match for the brew: sausages, onion rings, steamers, beer-battered fish and chips, and salads. The atmosphere is a bit Old World, but cleaner and better lit than the Hofbrauhaus ever was. And big enough to accommodate a macro crowd. (Call if you're not sure how to find the place; it's easy to get lost in this area.) *Lunch, dinner every day; AE, MC, V; local checks only; beer and wine.* ♿

PRESCOTT CAFE

6205 NE Prescott St
☎ (503) 287-8495
Northeast, Beyond 39th   ✗ Diner

The fare at Prescott Cafe is as homemade as homemade gets, and this eatery draws a steady stream of customers from the neighborhood and nearby mechanic shops as well as seniors and families throughout the day. A no-frills diner where coffee is the drink of choice and the jam pots are kept sparkling clean on every table, Prescott's offers a wide range of classic American breakfasts and lunches at incredibly reasonable prices. Two poached eggs on toast is exactly that. The huge pigs-in-a-blanket threatens to roll off the plate, and each pancake is so perfectly browned it could star in a movie. Bacon, ham, and linguisa sausage are the options for sides, as are huge stacks of pancakes and mounds of fluffy hashbrowns. The popular Prescott Quickie—an egg, cheese, and bacon muffin—plays second fiddle only to the fresh biscuits  and gravy, if the numbers of oohs and ahhs are any indication. Order a single blueberry pancake with the seafood omelet special and watch the server smile. Lunch features great hamburgers, chicken patty melts, BLTs, and a terrific fish sandwich with a perfectly deep-fried fillet. The turkey noodle soup—thick with homemade noodles and needing not a bit of salt or pepper—is probably better than Mom's. Desserts like airy lemon meringue, peach cobbler, and pumpkin pie are true specialties of the house—they often sell out before lunch is over. The servers know many of the regulars and warmly welcome newcomers. *Breakfast, lunch every day; no credit cards; checks OK; no alcohol.*

PRODUCE ROW CAFE

204 SE Oak St
☎ *(503) 232-8355*
Southeast, Close In　　　　　　　　　　　　　　　 *Pub Grub*

Surrounded by the warehouses and inner eastside factories of Portland, Produce Row Cafe keeps surviving because of its unique Portland setting, immense list of beers from around the world, late-night music, and a pool table known for the rather fierce competition it inspires. During the day the lunch menu does a solid trade with blue-collar workers from the neighbor-

hood. The dark interior with exposed rafters lends a slightly British pub feel, which ends at the food menu's offering of three big hero sandwiches on huge, fresh sourdough rolls or wheat bread. Rocky's Favorite is a wonderful classic (though served with mayonnaise and mustard) Italian sub composed of mortadella, Carriani, capacolla, cotto, and provolone. Polish sausage, eggplant, meatballs, and melts round out the hot sandwich choices. Red Eye Chili is another favorite, with or without the cheese and onions. Monday night jazz and Tuesday night bluegrass jam sessions draw supportive friends, music lovers, and hopeful musicians into the intimate warren of rooms that angle around the no-nonsense bar. Summertime finds the back deck filled with friends relaxing around pitchers under an open sky framed by the neighborhood's industrial walls as trains rattle past. *Lunch, dinner every day; no credit cards; checks OK; beer and wine.*

PUMPERNICKLES
344 NE 28th Ave
☎ *(503) 230-2349*
Laurelhurst ✕ *Coffeehouse*

Many who frequent this neighborhood cafe never even glance at the menu. Instead, they order their coffee at the counter and take in the lavish spread of homespun desserts and pastries—fruit cobblers, bread pudding, coffee cake, muffins, and cookies. While the sweets hold the greatest appeal, the "take out or hang out" menu delivers simple, honest fare: bagels and granola for breakfast; soup, salad, and sandwiches for lunch. Given the off-the-beaten-track location and expanded dining area, it's rarely crowded and often quiet; nearby residents can be found reading the paper from front to back page, refill after refill. *Breakfast, lunch every day; MC, V; checks OK; beer and wine.* ♿

RACCOON LODGE
7424 SW Beaverton-Hillsdale Hwy
☎ *(503) 296-0110*
Raleigh Hills ✕ *Pub Grub*

If you're one of those people who dine by cravings, the Raccoon Lodge (one of the latest additions to the Portland brewpub scene) offers one-stop shopping. For salty, there are the fries: shoestring, sweet potato, ale-battered, Yukon Gold, and tater tots, all served by the half or full bucket, with your choice of eight dipping sauces, like Creole tomato, raspberry habanero, and buttermilk ranch to name only a few. If it's a hamburger you're hankering after you won't be disappointed, but you will taxed when it comes to the choices: one-third, two-thirds, or a full pound? Cheddar, Swiss, or Jack? Caramelized onions, sautéed peppers, bacon, or "smokin' red-eye chili"? Other fixes worth indulging include the microbrews, a quaffable Bandit Amber, and an equally tasty Black Snout Stout, both brewed on the premises, and comfort food like meat loaf with buttermilk mashed potatoes or chocolate brownie pie. All of this upscale pub grub is served in a "lodge" surrounded by strip malls; though the  warmth of wood and Pendleton blanket-upholstered booths—not to mention the mounted elk head—lend a certain mountain charm, you'll never forget you're in the middle of the 'burbs. *Lunch, dinner every day; AE, MC, V; no checks; full bar.* ♿

RED COACH RESTAURANT

615 SW Broadway
☎ *(503) 227-4840*
Downtown   ✕ *American*

It's hard to beat the Red Coach when it comes to your basic hamburger setup. Nothing fancy, just the way you liked it as a kid—a thin patty on a toasted bun with melted American cheese, shredded lettuce, tomato and pickle slices, mayo, and bright yellow French's (no Dijon here, thank you very much) mustard. Add to that an order of fries and a frosty vanilla milk shake, or perhaps a cola. There's not much more to the menu, except variations on the burger (double patty? with bacon?), a sloppy joe, grilled cheese with tuna, and a perfect BLT (think crispy bacon and slathered with mayo). The original Red Coach opened in 1959 and moved (bringing booths, china, and menus) in 1985 to its present location in the light well of the Charles Berg building. The deep burgundy vinyl clam-shell booths and good old-fashioned (can you say genuinely friendly?) service is much appreciated. *Lunch Mon—Fri; no credit cards; no checks; no alcohol.* &

RED ELECTRIC CAFE

6440 SW Capitol Hwy
☎ *(503) 293-1266*
Hillsdale   ✕ *Soup/Salad/Sandwich*

This soup-and-sandwich roadside cafe redefines the genre: order a cup of creamy tomato soup and you'll find it comes with pesto-graced crostini. Put that cup of soup next to a grilled mozzarella and tomato sandwich on Grand Central's toasted Como bread, and you have an exciting, satisfying meal. And classics just get better with each new twist: the BLT comes with pesto mayo, while lingonberries sweeten the smoked turkey sandwich. The special of the day might be a sloppy joe or a meat loaf sandwich, and there's always a choice of cold beer or fresh lemonade to go along with the half-dozen varieties of burgers. Breakfasts—the standards—are delicious and hearty, with a long list of ingredients to choose from for the omelets. The once-close quarters were expanded in 1997; now there's room to spread out—and it still feels cozy. *Breakfast, lunch, dinner Mon—Sat; brunch Sun; MC, V; checks OK; beer and wine.* &

RIYADH'S

1318 SE Hawthorne Blvd
☎ *(503) 235-1254*
Hawthorne   ✕ *Middle Eastern*

If there's such thing as chickpea heaven, Riyadh's has a shoe in for its falafel. Freshly fried with a tender center, Riyadh's falafel ranks as one of Portland's best. Try it in a pita sandwich, have it as part of meze plate—or on a train or with a goat, you might eat it anywhere. And if falafel's not your thing, there are other sandwiches worth noting, like the feta cheese, grilled eggplant, or roasted vegetable, all handheld meals for under $4. Meat eaters can enjoy pita with chicken, beef, lamb, or *kafta* (ground, seasoned beef). Small plates and side dishes include lentil soup, cabbage rolls, stuffed grape leaves, and a spinach turnover. The steady stream of local lunchers overlook the worn linoleum and humble decor, focusing instead on the solid food, easy prices, and friendly counter service. A few well-chosen microbrews on tap and bottled Lebanese beers make for a pleasant surprise. *Lunch, dinner Mon–Sat; AE, DC, DIS, MC, V; checks OK; beer and wine.* ♿

ROCK BOTTOM RESTAURANT AND BREWERY

210 SW Morrison St
☎ *(503) 796-2739*
Downtown   ✕ *Pub Grub*

They boldly came west from Boulder, Colorado, with a gutsy idea: to establish a Rocky Mountain brewpub in the very city in Oregon known for starting the microbrew trend. Most Portlanders marveled at their audacity and doubted whether such outsiders could go up against such heavyweight homegrown competition as Portland Brewing Company, BridgePort, and Widmer. But Rock Bottom hasn't just survived in the last few years; it's thrived.

Beer lovers appreciate the brew and ambiance (billiards on the upper level, strategically placed TVs, a constant buzz); hungry shoppers and business people like the food, which runs the gamut from salads (try the vegetable-rich Mrs. Chow's) to sandwiches (the Brewer's Club is everything a club sandwich should be), to such exotics as buffalo fajitas. There's pasta, too, for those who cannot live

without it. To get the biggest bang for your buck, dine here for lunch; even then, prices may seem high—but the portions reflect it. *Lunch, dinner every day; AE, MC, V; local checks only; full bar.* &

SABURO'S
1667 SE Bybee Blvd
☏ *(503) 236-4237*
Westmoreland   ✕*Japanese*

What draws diners from all over the city to Saburo's is neither the vintage Naugahyde banquettes nor the shoebox feel to the place. And, Buddha knows, it's not the wait, which has become as integral to the experience as a wasabi rush. No, what makes Saburo's a destination for sushi lovers is this simple formula: consistently fresh fish, generous portions, fair prices. Everyone knows that sushi is rarely an option for budget diners; but practicing a certain amount of restraint, or ordering carefully prepared, delicious nonsushi items, yields happy bellies here. Combination dinners feature teriyaki, tempura, or gyoza, and come with salad, soup, rice, and ice cream; hovering around $10, these are very good values. Just bear in mind that the waiting list is consistently long because Saburo's is one of the best places in Portland to splurge on the raw stuff. *Dinner every day; AE, DC, MC, V; no checks; beer and wine.*

SAIGON KITCHEN
835 NE Broadway (and branch)
☏ *(503) 281-3669*
NE Broadway-Lloyd Center/SE Division   ✕ *Vietnamese/Thai*

The two branches of this restaurant are among the best of Portland's seemingly endless supply of Vietnamese eateries. The menu—more than 120 items long—features Thai dishes as well as the predominantly southern Vietnamese offerings. Standouts are the spicy soups—try the sour catfish concoction with pineapple—and the stews and ragouts, which go well with white or fried rice. Service is brisk and efficient at both busy locations. If the cheerful, enthusiastic waiters bring you a dish you didn't order, consider this: their unintentional error might be the perfect subliminal suggestion, because when it comes to expanding your food horizons, you can't go wrong here. Enjoy patio dining at the branch on SE Division: 3829 SE Division, (503) 236-2312. *Lunch, dinner every day; AE, DIS, MC, V; no checks; beer and wine.* &

SALVADOR MOLLY'S SUN SPOT CAFE

1523 SW Sunset Blvd
☎ (503) 293-1790
Hillsdale   ✗ Caribbean

Who'd have thought? A couple of years ago when it opened, Salvador
Molly's seemed little more than a bright spot in a tired little strip mall
off the Beaverton-Hillsdale Highway. But
before long, fans had passed the word
along that this place was outrageously
fun, and pretty soon the "dining room"
had spread outside to a charming covered balcony, and diners were queuing at
the door. They come for the new Latin
cuisine: Willapa Bay corn-crusted oyster

tacos, mouth-sizzling jerk grilled chicken, jambalayas studded with
shrimp and sausage, and the never-disappointing tamale of the day.
And they come for the mood, which is just plain good. Nobody's in a
hurry (and if you're in a hurry, you're sure to be disappointed), but
that's part of what makes this place happen. What's the rush? Sip a
margarita, crack a few peanuts, enjoy the wait. *Lunch, dinner
Mon–Sat; AE, DC, MC, V; checks OK; full bar.* ♿

SHANGHAI NOBLE HOUSE RESTAURANT

5331 SW Macadam Ave
☎ (503) 227-3136
SW Macadam Ave-Johns Landing   ✗ Chinese

Tucked away under the Water Tower at Johns Landing, the Shanghai
Noble House is impressively open and airy, with an opulent decor of
silken tapestries and multitiered Chinese lanterns. Though it specializes in Northern Szechwan cuisine, the Noble House has an extensive
and varied menu. Family dinners at $9.95 per person (of which there
are many versions, depending on the number in your party, as well as
an option to go spicy) include soup, spring rolls or pot stickers, several
entrees, rice, and tea. Or you can order a few dishes to share family-
style at the table; Lovers Birds Nest, featuring spicy General Tso's
chicken and shrimp in a crisp noodle "nest," or Shanghai Moo Shu
Chicken, a wrap of crumbled chicken breast and plum sauce in fresh
lettuce leaves, are some of the more unusual offerings. Venture beyond
a fortune cookie for dessert: try the homemade almond cookies or an
exotic treat such as the lychee or loquats served in a goblet on a bed of
ice. *Lunch, dinner every day; AE, MC, V; no checks; full bar.* ♿

SHANGHAI TUNNEL

211 SW Ankeny St
☎ *(503) 220-4001*
Old Town   ✗ *Lounge*

Shanghai Tunnel warms the hearts, souls, ears, and stomachs of folks
from every corner of Portland with its loud music and creatively struc-
tured menu. The restaurant has two long and narrow rooms: an
upstairs space with black booths and dim lighting,
and a downstairs basement bar. The former is a bit
quieter than the latter, but neither is conducive to
intimate conversation. The food is divine, though;
rarely does a bar serve such a variety of tasty and
creative morsels. A piping hot bowl of miso soup
served with jasmine rice and tofu costs only $3, and
a housemade black-bean burger with fries puts a
boring old Gardenburger to shame. Dare to be
wilder? Slurp down an order of Drunken Nudes,
super spicy noodles made with a glass of beer in mind. The booze is
also good, and the servers happily keep it flowing. No need to tote
your cigarettes along, as the bar is smoky enough that shallow to mod-
erate breathing should satiate any nicotine craving. *Dinner Tues– Sun;
MC, V; no checks; full bar.*

SIAM THAI

3800 Cedar Hills Blvd, Beaverton
☎ *(503) 626-6535*
Beaverton   ✗ *Thai*

In a horseshoe-shaped dining room that surrounds the kitchen, the
polite waiters at Siam serve up some of the best Thai food in the
97005 zip code—or any other Beaverton zip code for that matter.
Check the specials board for the fresh, high-quality salad rolls; made
with tofu, they taste good and they're good for you, too. (Pass on the
deep-fried spring rolls that appear on the menu, however.) By the time
entrees arrive, Siam really begins to shine: garlic beef is tender and
peppery, stir-fried with broccoli and sprinkled with cilantro; the red
curry is rich with coconut milk and textured with bamboo shoots.
phad thai, often a favorite of Americans, is a ketchupy-tasting disap-
pointment; go instead for the *phad khi-mao*, a wide-noodle dish seasoned with sweet basil and peppers. The menu offers wide variety
among very hot and mild dishes; and you can always cool your tongue
with Thai beer or mango juice. Siam gets busy, and when they do,

service can lag. But even then, a certain grace prevails—which is much appreciated in this part of a busy suburb. *Lunch, dinner every day; MC, V; no checks; beer and wine.* ♿

SKYLINE RESTAURANT
1313 NW Skyline Blvd
☎ *(503) 292-6727*
West Hills 🍴*Burgers*

Praised by the late food guru James Beard and country folk alike, this 65-year-old landmark has resisted change over the years. Servers have retained not only their hairdos from yesteryear, but also their commitment to providing good, old-fashioned service. Duct-tape patches cover the tears in the vinyl booths and black swivel stools, while gold-tone light fixtures illuminate the orange menus listing classic Americana: crispy fried chicken, fish and chips, a variety of burgers, grilled cheese sandwiches, thick and generous shakes, and soft-serve ice cream. Loved by both youngsters (who find it totally retro) and old-timers alike, it's a destination point on a Sunday drive. *Lunch, dinner every day; no credit cards; no checks; no alcohol.*

SOUTHPARK WINE BAR
919 SW Taylor St
☎ *(503) 326-1300*
Downtown 🍴*Wine Bar*

In 1998, when the Heathman Hotel announced plans to redo its beloved B. Moloch's on the south park blocks and turn it into a fussier full-fledged restaurant, we lamented; for years, it had been an easy downtown place to slip into for a glass of Widmer Hefeweizen and a quality pizza. Now we see we shouldn't have worried: the wine bar at Southpark is classy and inviting, and while you can still get a beer here, you might be more inclined to order a martini to go alongside your caramelized onion pizza or sip a glass of wine with a cheese plate or oysters on the half-shell. The menu in the wine bar is an abbreviated list from the main grill's menu and nothing runs over $10. While you will inevitably run up an expensive tab  eating in the restaurant, it's possible to watch your wallet and sup well on seafood like ceviche, or wood-fired mussels in the wine bar. Split a pizza and splurge on one the special desserts: choose the glorious bittersweet chocolate soufflé or the sour cherry bread pudding. *Lunch, dinner every day; AE, DC, DIS, MC, V; no checks; full bar.* &

STANICH'S

4915 NE Fremont (and branch)
☎ *(503) 281-2322*
Alameda-Beaumont/SW Macadam Ave-Johns Landing ✗ *Pub Grub*

From the time it opened in 1949, Stanich's has been a simple tavern that emphasizes sports, families, and burgers, and has resisted every trend since then. Located at the end of the Beaumont business district, locals and families relax over pitchers of Bud-weiser or Cokes while waiting for the short-order cook to fry up a classic American burger. Served in paper-covered plastic baskets, these burgers vary in their toppings—all are served with lettuce, tomato, and fresh onion—with options to add a fried egg, bacon strips, or a slab of ham. The seri-ously famished have them all stacked together—a huge heart-stopping burger encased in a perfectly crisped bun. For a buck extra per order you can have fries, too, loved by the regulars for their simple greasy potatoness. Felt pennant flags from what looks like every college and professional team in the 50 states cover the tavern walls; ask if you can't find where your favorite team's has been placed. Above the barstools overlooking the cook's grill hangs the modest TV. Mercifully, it doesn't blare no matter what game is on; you are more likely to hear the hum of diners' talk and laughter. Same menu, less history at Stanich's West in Johns Landing (5627 SW Kelly St; 503/246-5040). *Lunch, dinner Mon–Sat; no credit cards; no checks; beer and wine.* &

STEPPING STONE

2390 NW Quimby St
☎ *(503) 222-1132*
Northwest ✗ *Breakfast*

There's an appealing throwback feeling to this place, something that reminds you of the time before Microsoft, before Gen X, before a cap-puccino was something you could find as readily as a Coca Cola. (Okay, okay: a sandwich board out front proclaims that espresso is available here, but we've never even heard the whoosh of a steamer at Stepping Stone.) Maybe it's the room decor, well-worn and efficient, with a long counter and spinning stools and enough tables to seat just about anyone who comes by: slackers, business people, students. Maybe, too, it's the very affordable food; you'll find such standbys as oatmeal, pancakes, and eggs, eggs, eggs—in omelets, poached on toast, or as an early riser special (from 6am to 9am) for $2.75. Whatever the appeal, Stepping Stone, next door to a tiny salon and within easy walking distance to bustling NW 23rd Avenue, has been doing its thing a long time. Probably you'll wear out before it does. *Breakfast, lunch Tues–Sun; no credit cards; local checks OK; no alcohol.*

STICKERS ASIAN CAFE

6808 SE Milwaukie Ave
☎ *(503) 239-8739*
Westmoreland   ✗ *Pan-Asian*

John Sinclair and Joan Francis spent several years in China eating different regional variations of pot stickers, the quintessential Sino street food. Now at their restaurant Stickers they cook and serve this and other snack foods of Asia. Located on what has become the hot yuppie food corner of Westmoreland, the beautiful, artful surroundings belie the remarkably affordable prices for food that is grandly conceived and near perfectly executed. The menu does not confine itself to China, roaming down to India and over to Thailand, but never feeling like contrived "Pan-Asian." The hot and sour soup with pot stickers is much thinner than what you might be used to from your corner Chinese place and more delicately fla-

vored—and it's all for the better. The cold sesame noodle salad is refreshing and snappy, not heavily saturated with sesame oil. Double Happiness, the happy hour special for $4.50, consists of a plate of six pot stickers with the traditional dipping sauce (the best and most balanced mix we've had of vinegar, soy, ginger, garlic, and chile) and a well drink. Double indeed, and then some. *Dinner every day; MC, V; checks OK; full bar.* ♿

SUPER BURRITO EXPRESS

9019 N Lombard St (and branch)
☎ *(503) 283-2181*
St. Johns/Milwaukie   ✗ *Mexican*

If you're looking for something notable at this burrito quick-stop, look past the patio furniture and old, worn booths to the food. For less money than a Sunday paper and cappuccino, you can dine here on *chile relleno* burritos ($2.95); home-made and flavorful chicken, beef, or pork tamales ($1.10); spicy carne asade tacos; and cheesy quesadillas with pastrami and chiles ($2.50). With a reputation for cheap, filling, and quick, there's sometimes a long line to order food at these popular lunch

hangouts, but every effort is made to remain true to the promise of "express." *Menudo*, the Mexican dish of tripe and hominy, is served on Saturdays and Sundays at the St. Johns location. (With the recent facelift to the neighborhood, there are many shops to stroll through while you're in the area. Or in sunny weather take your lunch to Cathedral Park, under the St. Johns Bridge along the Willlamette River.) Check out the Milwaukie location, too: 4210 SE King Road, (503) 786-9370. *Lunch, dinner every day; AE, MC, V; no checks; no alcohol.*

SURIYA THAI

1231 SW Washington St
☎ *(503) 228-5775*
Downtown   ✗ *Thai*

A pink-walled, teddy bear–adorned dining room may seem an unlikely place for Thai food, but at Suriya that's just what you get—and with food this reliable, you could get used to the decor pretty quickly. Lunch specials, including such non-Thai dishes as yakisoba, are served with a delicious tomato-based soup at an affordable $5.50. Dinner, however, may be the best time to eat here. Standbys such as the *tom kha gai* (chicken soup with coconut milk, lemongrass, and galangal root) and phad thai (fried rice noodles with shrimp, egg, green onions, and ground peanuts) are always good; another noodle dish to try is the spicy-sweet basil noodles. Other Thai restaurants in Portland serve a broader variety of entrees and are perhaps more adventuresome in their use of spice, but for Thai food downtown, Suriya is a good bet. And, if you can't abide the teddy bears, there's always takeout. *Lunch, dinner Mon–Sat; AE, DIS, MC, V; local checks OK; beer and wine.* &

SUSHI TAKAHASHI

24 NW Broadway (and branch)
☎ *(503) 224-3417*
Downtown/Southeast, Beyond 39th   *Japanese*

The most compelling reason to visit this downtown sushi spot? The Train. At Sushi Takahashi, most of the seats circle around the large oval sushi bar laid with train track. As the sushi-laden miniature train makes its rounds, diners pull off as many plates as their hearts—or stomachs—desire. At the end of the meal a waitperson counts the plates and writes out a bill. This is definitely an alternative to the more elite sushi houses—especially when it comes to the cost—just don't expect really exquisite sushi. The sushi guys here bang out the food, and the prices reflect their no-nonsense approach. On Wednesday evenings and Saturdays at lunch and dinner, prices dip even lower than usual; most plates with two pieces of sushi are only $1.25. Special sushi items are more expensive, but you can eat more sushi per dollar here than at any other place in Portland. And though you don't have to be a kid to get a kick out of the train, the special delivery system makes this an especially appealing experience for children. (At the original Takahashi—10324 SE Holgate Street, 503/760-8135—the train offers only visual amusement, not delivery service.) *Lunch, dinner Mon–Sat; MC, V; no checks; beer and wine.* ⓖ

SUZANNE'S AT BEAUMONT VILLAGE

3517 NE 46th Ave
☎ *(503) 282-4233*
Alameda-Beaumont   ✗ *Cafe*

Walking into this cute little restaurant, one feels a bit like Alice In Wonderland when she was in her tall phase. Tiny tables with perky orange napkins, floral wallpaper, and light from south-facing windows all add to the cheery tea-party ambiance. Along with the tried-and-true standards, the breakfast menu offers ethnic exotica such as Swedish crêpes with lingonberries; croissant halves grilled like French toast and drizzled with raspberry-orange sauce; and *piperade basquaise*—a savory mélange of sautéed sweet peppers, tomato, and onion, topped with scrambled eggs and smoked ham. Buttermilk biscuits and honey butter make a wondrous morning combination, and the freshly squeezed orange juice meets the standard these breakfasts set. At lunch, soup or salad and a tiny basket of bread grace your table alongside your choice of entree from the simple menu, which features a trio of sandwiches, home-made daily quiche, shrimp salad, and lemon chicken caesar. Spinach salad arrives jutting with orange slices, studded with real bacon and mushrooms, wanting only a zestier dressing. Save room for one of indulgences from the ever-changing dessert list; choices range from a dense berry chocolate cake and an elegant lemon curd tart to sea-sonal pies. *Breakfast, lunch Tues–Sat; AE, DIS, MC, V; checks OK; no alcohol.* &

SWAGAT
4325 SW 109th Ave, Beaverton (and branch)
☎ *(503) 626-3000*
Beaverton/Northwest   ✕ *Indian*

This Beaverton tract house across from Target looks like it should pro-duce Rice Krispies Treats, not great Indian food. But somehow, people enter the door and—at least spiritually—never leave. Moving from pil-lowy *dosas*—giant lentil pancakes wrapped around a filling of curry—diners slip eagerly into tandoori dishes with a barbecue bite; spinach *paneer* laced with cheese cubes and fire; or a spicy, buttery Chicken Makhani. It's hard to spend much money here even at dinner, and the lunch buffet—featuring pakoras, vegetable curries, some kind of vindaloo, *naan*, chutneys, raita, salad, and warm cardamom-scented rice pudding—is one of the best deals in town. The vindaloos may be vibrant, but the atmosphere is low-key; the feeling is Beaverton, not Bengal. If you're looking for

atmosphere, a large, flashy outpost that opened a couple of years ago on Portland's NW 21st Avenue at Lovejoy (2074 NW Lovejoy Street; 503/227-4300) has ambiance as hot as its tandoor. *Lunch, dinner every day; AE, DIS, MC, V; checks OK; beer and wine (full bar in the Northwest location).* &

SWEETWATER'S JAM HOUSE
3350 SE Morrison St
☎ *(503) 233-0333*
Belmont   ✕ *Caribbean*

After starting out in a tiny outpost in the Hollywood district, this lively Caribbean spot moved to larger (and unquestionably cooler) digs in the refurbished Belmont Dairy. In the process it's lost none of its fire—peppered shrimp and goat curry still cauterize your taste buds—or its fun, with terrific barbecued ribs; jerk chicken; and zippy, fruity chicken skewers. Sides are stunning, from dark, molasses-infused corn bread to ethereal coconut rice or "smashed" potatoes, and three of them (including the not-for-Thanksgiving curried pumpkin) come together for the veggie-flashy Rastafarian plate. There is also an extensive shelf of Caribbean rums, and a wicked list of things the bar does with them. *Dinner every day; AE, DC, DIS, MC, V; no checks; full bar.* &

TACO DEL MAR

3106 SE Hawthorne Blvd (and branches)
☎ *(503) 232-7763*
Hawthorne/Downtown/Southeast, Close In   ✗ *Mexican*

For a no-frills, non-yuppiefied, regular-Joe fish burrito, this chain taqueria delivers. The menu board lists an array of land-animal bur-ritos and tacos, but face it: the raison d'être lies in the big, fat Super Fish Burrito—especially if you add avocado and sour cream. Loaded with freshly fried white fish, shredded cabbage, zippy tartar sauce, salsa, refried or whole beans, and, if you choose—don't do it!—shredded cheese, this burrito can slay the hungriest appetite. (And, should you wane partway through, they're not bad reheated.) Those with smaller appetites can, of course, order a regular-sized fish burrito. The smaller, soft fish tacos, with just one slab of fish, are popular with kids. Customer loyalty and 10 punches on your burrito card nets you one free burrito; you get double punches on Mondays. There's not much in the way of seating or ambiance, unless you like neon wall signs, a string of light bulbs, traffic noise, and tiny tables. Other locations in Portland are 433  SW Fourth Avenue, (503) 226-0507; 923 SW Oak Street, (503) 827-3040; 438 SE MLK Jr. Boulevard, (503) 232-7695; and 736 SW Taylor Street, (503) 827-8311. *Lunch, dinner every day; no credit cards; checks OK; no alcohol.* &

TALESI THAI CUISINE

2014 NE Broadway
☎ *(503) 331-1235*
NE Broadway-Lloyd Center   ✗ *Thai*

NE Broadway is a good bet for those on the prowl for a good, reason-ably priced meal. Here, family establishments abound, with predictable variations in quality and style. Talesi is one of several Thai restaurants on Broadway, and is a solid choice for carefully prepared food in a warm, old-house atmosphere without a trace of the kitschy Thai decor found elsewhere. The menu covers standard Thai dishes such as chicken satay, barbecued chicken, curries,

and phad thai (hold the ketchup!), but breaks out of the mold with excellent specials like deep-fried pompano (a delicate tropical fish) in a variety of spicy sauces; shrimp and squid in a firey, minty sauce; and Talesi curry with roasted duck, tomatoes, and basil leaves. The appetizer, soup, and salad menus list some interesting and unfamiliar selections (*larb*, anyone?); try something new for an eventful and delicious meal. *Tom yum goong*, a spicy and sour shrimp soup, is especially satisfying. A good place for a quiet conversation, a Singha, and food that you won't find just anywhere, Talesi is relaxed and homey, right down to the service. *Lunch Mon–Fri, dinner every day; MC, V; no checks; beer and wine.* &

THE TAO OF TEA

3430 SE Belmont St
☏ *(503) 736-0119*
Belmont   ✗ *Teahouse*

In the yin-yang cycle of life, sipping tea out of a ceramic vessel to the sound of trickling water is the natural antidote to sucking coffee out of a paper cup to the backdrop of an accelerating motor. The Tao of Tea, a pretty little tea room bedecked with colorful cushions and tea-lined walls, offers sweet respite from the chaos of modern life. Meditative and wistful describes the ambiance, enhanced by the ceremony of simple tea service; here what cup you drink out of has everything to do with the tea you ordered: green, black, white, scented, oolong, or herbal. All the food offerings, a range of Eastern flavors from Chinese pot stickers to fried Japanese tofu and Indian dal with rice, go well with a pot of tea; the flatbreads with chutneys are especially good. Though a pot of tea will cost you more here than anyplace else in town, most of the substantial offerings average between $5 and $8. And when it comes to your mental health, it's hardly worth scrimping. *Lunch, dinner every day. DIS, MC, V; checks OK; no alcohol.* &

TAQUERIA CHAVEZ

5703 SE 82nd Ave
☎ *(503) 777-2282*
Southeast, Beyond 39th ✗ *Mexican*

Sandwiched between a McDonald's and a used-car lot, this unas-suming taqueria makes authentic Mexican food: hand-patted tortillas and knock-your-sombrero-off chili sauces that warm the heart and stomach lining. A choice of *birria* (a deliciously spiced and tender shredded beef), *chorizo* (sausage), tongue, pork, or chicken fill the small tacos that are topped with onions and cilantro. Rely on the person behind the counter to guide you through the menu past the familiar burritos—which, though good, don't compare to the tamales. Mexican kitsch—black velvet paintings and strings of plastic peppers— as well as colorful blankets and garlic braids, attempt to camouflage the need for fresh paint in the small dining room of four tables plus counter seating. *Lunch, dinner every day; no credit cards; no checks; no alcohol.*

TAQUERIA EL VALE

5832 NE Glisan St
☎ *(503) 235-5268*
Northeast, Beyond 39th ✗ *Mexican*

Patriotism abounds with two Mexican flags hanging on opposite walls, the local Spanish-speaking station broadcasted from the corner television, and Coke and Crush served in Mexican-made bottles. Home of the huge and satisfying $2.50 burrrito, Tacqueria El Vale offers you a wide range of fillings and combinations: beans, rice, cilantro, onions, tomatoes, *chorizo*, scrambled eggs, *chiles rellenos*, and shredded beef. Other options include tacos (at a dollar apiece) filled with various meats, several different kinds of quesadillas, tamales (pork, chicken, or beef), vegetarian tostadas ($1.50), and a number of combination plates. Though at first glance the menu may seem intimidating with its many less-than-familiar ingredients, rely on the friendly counter help for assistance. There's also a glossary on the back of the menu that defines about 50 terms you may encounter when ordering Mexican food, like *menudo* (tripe and hominy soup, served here Fridays and Saturdays), *pozole* (chicken or pork soup with hominy), and *guisado* (a stew

of beef or pork with vegetables). *Lunch, dinner every day; no credit cards; checks OK; no alcohol.* &

TARA THAI NORTHWEST

1310 NW 23rd Ave
☎ *(503) 222-7840*
Northwest ✗ *Thai/Laotian*

There used to be three branches of this family-run Thai restaurant, but now there is only one; in 1998 owner Lavanny Phommaneth sold the Beaverton and Tigard restaurants in order to channel her time and energy into the Northwest location. Oh, the lucky residents of this neighborhood! Everything about this converted former home is pleasant: the modest but comfortable dining room, the understated but knowledgeable servers, the wonderfully fresh and flavorful food. The menu concentrates on the foods of Northern Thailand and Laos, which translates into such recognizable dishes as fresh salad rolls, *tom kai kai* (ginger-coconut milk soup with chicken), green curry, and phad thai, as well as less familiar Lao specialties: *khao poon nam kai* (a delicious chicken-rice noodle soup flavored with fresh banana leaves, basil, and galangal) and *soop pak* (steamed vegetables in a roasted ginger paste). For dessert there's a murky gray—but nonetheless tasty—rice pudding with bananas, and, in season, mangoes over sweet sticky rice in coconut milk. *Lunch, dinner everyday; AE, DC, DIS, MC, V; no checks; beer and wine.* &

TENNESSEE RED'S

2133 SE 11th Ave (and Branch)
☎ *(503) 231-1710*
Southeast, Close In/SE Powell ✗ *Barbecue*

You can smell this southeast Portland storefront a block away—the question is, which of five barbecue sauces are you smelling? With its powerful smoke pits, Tennessee Red's can gild chicken, beef and pork ribs, pork loin, and brisket with Texas, Carolina, Memphis, and Arkansas sauces—or an Oregon version with hazelnuts. The meat is juicy and deeply smoky, and the possible sides extend from corn bread to beans and rice to intense mashed potatoes. There are also a number of ambitious barbecue sandwiches, which require hearty appetites and large hands—and a certain indifference to the cleanliness of your shirt. Most of the barbecue heads out the door, but if basic tables and chairs and lots of aroma fit your idea of ambiance, you can consume your barbecue before it even thinks about cooling down. The second location at SE 82nd Avenue and Powell Boulevard serves breakfast and has a full bar. *Lunch, dinner Mon–Sat; MC, V; local checks only; beer.* &

THAI LITTLE HOME

3214 E Fourth Plain Blvd, Vancouver, WA
☎ *(360) 693-4061*
Vancouver, WA and Vicinity   ✕ *Thai*

It's not as fancy as similar joints across the river in Portland, but here Serm Pong and his family prepare fresh, homecooked Thai food that Vancouver locals like just fine. *Yum nuer* (sliced beef salad with cucumber, seasoned with chile and lime juice) rivals the popular *pra koong* (shrimp with chili paste, lemongrass, and lime juice); and the appetizers like *mee krob* (crisp Thai noodles) and

chicken satay are something to write home about. Service is friendly, informed, and fast. *Lunch Mon–Fri, dinner Mon–Sat; AE, MC, V; local checks only; beer and wine.*

THAI ORCHID

2231 W Burnside St (and branches)
☎ *(503) 226-4542*
Northwest/Multnomah/Vancouver, WA and Vicinity/
West Linn   ✕ *Thai*

It's a weekday evening, but a stream of glossy, youthful Portlanders flow into this low-profile Burnside storefront—probably for the Evil Jungle Noodles. Owners Na and Penny Saenguraiporn consistently produce reasonably priced and more than reasonably spiced Thai food. The place looks so mild, you may be surprised by both the size of the menu and the food's powers of heat generation—a fact not lost on faithful takeout customers. Entrees, especially a seafood in chili sauce and a deep-fried whole fish, tend to be more interesting than appetizers. The beef salad is pungent and mouth-clearing—and now it's clearing mouths throughout the Metropolitan area with outposts on SW Barbur Boulevard, in West Linn, and in Vancouver. *Lunch Mon–Fri, dinner every day; AE, DIS, MC, V; checks OK; beer and wine.* &

THAI TOUCH CUISINE

4806 SE Stark
☎ *(503) 230-2875*
Southeast, Beyond 39th ✗ *Thai*

Thai Touch looks like a lot of other Thai restaurants in Portland: a bevy of banquet chairs, wall-to-wall carpet, and a modest attempt at decorating. This lack of ambiance, however, is compensated by exciting cooking. One taste of the red curry—tender chicken in a spicy broth of chile-infused coconut milk—or the drunken noodles, and you'll wonder why you haven't been here before. The menu is quite long, listing both the familiar (*tom kah*, phad thai, green curry) and the vernacular, such as The Ocean, a spicy medley of shellfish and vegetables. Lunch is a good bargain: for $3.95 you choose one of four, plus an appetizer, and soup or salad. *Lunch, dinner Tues–Sun; MC, V; no checks; no alcohol.* ♿

THAI VILLA

340 N 1st St, Lake Oswego
☎ *(503) 635-6164*
Lake Oswego ✗ *Thai*

The heat thermometer here ranges from "calm" to "volcano" (with little in between). A popular Lake Oswego restaurant, Thai Villa specializes in fiery, pungent soups and a wide range of seafood dishes. The chef is handy with basil, garlic, and subtle hints of sweetness, and the prices are reasonable, especially on a cost-per-tingle basis. It's a good thing this place sits near the Lake Oswego fire department, because someday someone is going to take an innocent bite of "volcano" *gang galee* (chicken curry with potatoes) and self-combust. *Lunch Mon–Fri, dinner every day; DIS, MC, V; no checks; beer and wine.*

THANH THAO

4005 SE Hawthorne Blvd (and branch)
☎ *(503) 238-6232*
Hawthorne/SE Powell ✗ *Thai/Vietnamese*

This Hawthorne-area Thai/Vietnamese restaurant does a brisk takeout business, which may be the way to go, since getting a table is no easy work. It's also a good place to be a regular, because that's the only way you'll work your way through the extensive menu before the year 2008. Some of the food is very good: on the short Thai menu the chicken coconut soup, punctuated with snow peas, mushrooms, and bites of chicken, is silky smooth; and the phad thai, topped with crunchy bean sprouts and bits of peanuts, is fine (in fact, noodle dishes—Thai or Vietnamese—are usually a sure bet). You'll find some ordinary dishes here (like peanut chicken), but all are generous. In the realm of more exotic fare, the menu satisfies with such delicacies as squid with pineapple, tomatoes, mushrooms, and celery, and a curried goat dish. There's a second branch at 8355 SE Powell Boulevard; (503) 775-0306. *Lunch, dinner Wed–Mon; AE, MC, V; checks OK; beer and wine.*

TK'S SMOKEHOUSE & BBQ CO

12810 NW Cornell Rd
☎ *(503) 626-2226*
Oak Hills   ✕ *Barbecue*

Owner Tomiko Warren says the T stands for Tomiko and, depending on the day, K stands for either her middle name, Kristina, or her husband's name, Kevin. One look at the menu will tell you that every day BBQ stands for a range of possibilities. With seven sauces, including the searing Red Hot Ruby and the smokyish Dad's sauce, TK's serves up enough variety to please just about anyone. Choose from pork, beef, and chicken barbecue; sausages; blackened catfish; or Gardenburgers, all priced from $4.75 to $13.95.

Of almost a dozen sides—two come with dinner—we like the collard greens and the mashed potatoes. If you make it through all that, the desserts will tempt you: maybe Key lime or buttermilk pies, or something called Wicked Wicked Fudge Cake. For years before she quit her government job and opened a restaurant,  Tomiko Warren had cooked backyard barbecue for her neighbors. At TK's you get the feeling that's what she's still up to—one table at a time. TK's can be hard to find; it's between Murray Street and Saltzmen Road in the farthest western reaches of the city. *Breakfast Sat–Sun, lunch, dinner Tues–Sun; AE, DC, DIS, MC, V; local checks only; beer and wine.* ♿

TONEY BENTO
1423 SE 37th Ave
☎ *(503) 234-4441*
Hawthorne   ✕*Japanese*

This little spot just off of Hawthorne Boulevard has the feel that
Macheezmo Mouse had way back when, only rather than being decon-
structed Mexican, it's reconstructed Asian.
Loud and eclectic means the plucked guitars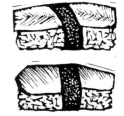
of the latest indie-rock, not the plucked,
classical strings of the Koto. The pierced and
dyed counter staff is friendly enough to
appease the more culturally timid, and
starving artists and college students will
appreciate the very cheap food. Where else
can you get a large bowl of miso soup with
udon noodles for $2.75? Numerous bento bowls (in the $4 to $5
range) combine various ingredients—both vegetable and animal—with
mountains of sticky white rice. The accompanying sauces are right-on
but not hyperactive with flavor; this can be modified to your heart's
content at the impressive circular condiment center. No less than 12
different sauces and unctuants make their appearance on this Lazy
Susan of Delight. People have been known to go plum (sauce) crazy
here, taking multiple little dishes of these concoctions just because
they can. *Lunch, dinner every day; AE, DIS, MC, V; checks OK; beer
and wine.* ⚹

1201 CAFE AND LOUNGE
1201 SW 12th Ave
☎ *(503) 225-1201*
Downtown   ✕*Lounge*

The 1201 sits in the ground floor of a large, faceless office building in
a part of downtown between Portland State University and the commercial district that has little character. Once you've opened the heavy
red doors and entered the smoky interior of this lounge, however,
you're immediately subject to loads of personality; for some, perhaps,
too much. This is a bar with an eclectic range of music, from blaring
punk rock to crooning Frank Sinatra, and the dyed hair flames.
Thursday through Saturday there's live music that's sometimes head-
banging, sometimes soft and twangy. The swanky, dark red velvet
interior is classic cocktail lounge, the perfect backdrop for sipping a
Manhattan or martini. For food, the caesar salad and soups stand

out, while the pastas tend to be heavy. If you like Dots and Bar of the Gods, but you want a real drink, this is the place. *Lunch, dinner every day; MC, V; no checks; full bar.* ♿

TYPHOON!

2310 NW Everett St (and branch)
☎ *(503) 243-7557*
Northwest/Downtown   *Thai*

Chef and owner Bo Kline does a Thai cuisine with more colors than curry. From openers of *miang kam* (fresh spinach leaves wrapped around a half-dozen ingredients) and beggar's purses of succulent shrimp, the menu offers a kaleidoscope of curries, inspired seafood entrees, and pungent noodle dishes. (The King's Noodles, with chicken and most of the spices you can think of, has fanatic devotees.) Kline has a particularly deft hand with shrimp and fish, allowing the seafood's delicate flavors to surmount ginger, garlic, basil, and some spices that could cook a flounder by themselves. The atmosphere is hipper than that of many Thai restaurants, with colorful *Bopla!* plates decorating each place setting, and an indoor-outdoor option when the weather allows. The restaurant also offers 70 different teas at the northwest location (and 150 at the Broadway location)—but with these chiles, you might want to stick to beer. The new second location, Typhoon! On Broadway (400 SW Broadway, 503/224-8285), has found a home in the Imperial Hotel and provides a more spacious and sophisticated setting for dining on the same exciting flavors. *Lunch Mon–Sat, dinner every day; AE, DC, MC, V; no checks; beer and wine (full bar on Broadway).* ♿

VISTA SPRING CAFE

2430 SW Vista Ave
☎ *(503) 222-2811*
West Hills   🍴 *Pizza*

Portland Heights residents pack this place for gourmet pizzas, microbrews, lushiously thick milk shakes, sandwiches, or pasta. Even if the pies lack some of the spark that pizza fiends have learned to expect in recent years, the crust is tasty and they're loaded with all the right toppings: olives, prosciutto, Thai chicken, sun-dried tomatoes, feta cheese. The red-ceilinged, low-lit room has a velvety feeling—with booths along the

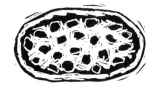

walls and strings of twinkling lights hung about. A welcoming spot with nice folks, too, it's the quintessential neighborhood cafe. *Lunch, dinner every day; DIS, MC, V; checks OK; beer and wine.* ♿

THE WESTERN CULINARY INSTITUTE
1316 SW 13th Ave
☎ *(503) 294-9770*
Downtown   ✗ *International*

For true food adventurers who place a higher value on the unexpected and inexpensive rather than the polished and flamboyant, this dining room, a classroom fashioned as a restaurant for students of the Western Culinary Institute, offers some of the most creative meals for the least amount of money in Portland. All the food is prepared on site by students and tends toward French classics such as consommé, crêpes, roulade, with nods toward current trends (caesar salad, wild greens, a polenta "sandwich"). At lunch there are three menu choices: a la carte, three-course for $5.95, and seven-course at $7.95 (which, for those of you inclined toward mathematical equations, is little more that a buck a course). And the food is good. A three-course meal might start with the *Vol au Vent* appetizer, a puff pastry shell stuffed with a tangy blend of fresh marinated vegetables and feta cheese paired with simply dressed mixed greens, then follow with *Supremes de Volaille a la Milanese*—breaded, sautéed chicken medallions served with a lively tomato sauce. Heavenly finishes include a praline crème caramel, flourished with candied pecans, spun sugar, and an orange honey sauce. What the service lacks in experience, it more than makes up for in earnestness and food knowledge—after all, the servers are all culinary students, not professional waiters; do listen to their recommendations when choosing from the menu. Framed travel posters are the only attempt at decorating an otherwise sparse room of banquet chairs, white tablecloths, and green wall-to-wall carpet. Keep your eyes focused on the food before you, and order a glass of wine to wash away the feeling that you're all just playing restaurant. *Lunch, dinner Tues—Fri; MC, V; no checks; beer and wine only.*

WIDMER GASTHAUS

955 N Russell St
☎ *(503) 281-3333*
North Portland   *Pub Grub*

The careful craftsmanship that raised Widmer Brewing from two yeasty rooms in northwest Portland to a nationally known maxi-microbrew surfaces in both the cooking and the restoration of this industrial area hangout. The old Albina relic of a building is now a haven of polished wood, copper, and glass, and the dining space keeps growing. The food is simple German and American— sausages, sauerbraten, goulash, and thick sandwiches—but it's tasty and substantial. The atmosphere is equally warm, and both the cuisine and the ambiance benefit considerably from a six-beer sampler, in miniature mugs,  extending from *Schwarzbier* to fruity Widberry. Your crowd might want to think of the minis as the appetizer, with a pitcher of lemon-laced Hefeweizen as the entree. *Lunch, dinner every day; AE, DIS, MC, V; local checks only; beer and wine.* &

WOODSTOCK WINE AND DELI

4030 SE Woodstock Blvd
☎ *(503) 777-2208*
Woodstock   *Deli*

Back in the mid-1980s, when owners Tak and Sue Fujino set up shop, this part of southeast Portland was a sleepy, working-class neighborhood with a distinctly small-town feel. Though times have changed and the boulevard now bustles, the deli remains one of the city's best-kept secrets, serving up an irresistible combination of gourmet food in a laid-back setting. For lunch or an early dinner, try the excellent lasagne with spicy Italian sausage, creamy Gorgonzola pasta salad, or the tasty Greek salad festooned with green, red, and yellow peppers. The deli also offers a tempting variety of sandwiches and a small but impressive selection of imported and local beer. An expansion in the early '90s added more tables and chairs and the Great Wall of Wine, a treasure-trove for oenophiles and oenophytes alike. And there are lots of tempting takehome goodies—salami, olives, cheese, truffles—to go with your bottled purchase. *Lunch, early dinner Mon–Sat; MC, V; checks OK; beer and wine.*

WU'S OPEN KITCHEN

17773 SW Lower Boones Ferry Rd, Lake Oswego (and branch)
☎ *(503) 636-8899*
Lake Oswego/Tigard ✕ *Chinese*

The flames leaping high behind the windows in the back of the restaurant are firing the large woks in the kitchen, and you can watch the cooks deftly preparing dishes while you wait for dinner. Chef Jimmy Wu's extended family helps run this place, serving a variety of spicy and not-so-spicy dishes from all over China (but the cooks pander to the American palate; consequently the hot dishes won't wilt too many taste buds). Seafood is fresh, vegetables are crisp, sauces are light, and service is speedy and attentive. Kids will feel right at home, and parents will appreciate the modest prices. Prepare for a wait on weekends—Wu's is popular with locals. There is a second restaurant in Tigard (12180 SW Scholls Ferry Road, 503/579-8899). *Lunch, dinner every day; DIS, MC, V; no checks; full bar.* ♿

YEN HA

6820 NE Sandy Blvd
☎ *(503) 287-3698*
Northeast, Beyond 39th ✕ *Vietnamese*

With 160 items, Portland's most extensive Vietnamese menu (and one of its oldest) offers a range of possibilities that invite exploration. You might try a messy, tangy whole Dungeness crab ($19.95 for four people), a game hen with coconut rice, or one of the remarkable preparations of frogs' legs. Some local Vietnamese have been heard to mutter that the menu (and the spicing) has become a bit Americanized, but the crowd is consistently multicultural. The ambiance is Formica and Budweiser, with karaoke in the bar. *Lunch, dinner every day; AE, MC, V; no checks; full bar.* ♿

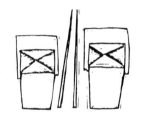

ZELL'S CAFE

1300 SE Morrison St
☎ *(503) 239-0196*
Southeast, Close In ✕ *Breakfast*

Since the departure of founder Tom Zell in 1996, Judith Sacheck has brought some welcome changes to this neighborhood breakfast mecca—namely, Bloody Marys and eggs Benedict. The fresh fruit waffles, range of pancakes (try the ginger if they're available), and inspired egg dishes (such as the trademark *chorizo*-and-peppers omelet and, if you're lucky, scrambled eggs with smoked salmon, Gruyère, and green onions) are as reliable as ever. Expect a warm welcome here, even on chilly weekend mornings when you may be forced to wait outside for a table: the awning is outfitted with heating elements, and you can get a hot cup of coffee and a heartening view of the feathery scones. Of course there is a lunch menu, with thick burgers, vegetarian sandwiches, and fresh fish specialties, but the breakfasts are tough to beat. *Breakfast, lunch every day; AE, DIS, MC, V; checks OK; beer, wine, and selected liquor.*

ZIEN HONG

5314 NE Sandy Blvd
☎ *(503) 288-4743*
Northeast, Beyond 39th   ✕ *Chinese*

It's a wonder there aren't more traffic accidents on NE Sandy Boulevard near 53rd Avenue, because the smells wafting from Zien Hong warrant immediate braking action. A longtime fixture of the neighborhood, this is one of Portland's most authentic Chinese eateries (though the Monet prints on the wall aren't exactly evocative of Asia). Starting with the salad rolls and hot and sour soup and going right through to the milk shake–like coconut concoctions, this is the real Mao. Vegetarian selections are okay—most notable is the broccoli in spicy garlic sauce—but the kitchen really shines with its meat-based dishes. Don't leave without trying the pepper-salted shrimp (worth fighting over who gets the last one), the sizzling beef and scallops, or the ginger chicken. On busy nights, don't expect your food to arrive immediately. Lunch specials are a good deal, with soup of the day and steamed rice accompanying an entree; all are less than $5. *Lunch, dinner every day; AE, MC, V; no checks; beer and wine.*

location index
portland neighborhoods

Riyadh's
Taco del Mar
Thanh Thao
Toney Bento

HILLSDALE
Garbonzos
Goldberg's Bakery
Nature's Marketplace
Noah's New York Bagels
Pizzicato
Red Electric Cafe
Salvador Molly's Sun Spot Cafe

LAURELHURST
L'il Mexico Restaurant
Laurelthirst Public House
Nature's Marketplace
Pizzicato
Pumpernickles

MULTNOMAH
Fat City Cafe
Grand Central Bakery and Cafe
Marco's Cafe and Espresso Bar
Thai Orchid

NE BROADWAY–LLOYD CENTER
Aztec Willie & Joey Rose Taqueria
Cadillac Cafe
Chez Jose East
Colosso
Grand Central Bakery and Cafe
Macheezmo Mouse
Marsee Baking
Pizza Luna
Saigon Kitchen
Talesi Thai Cuisine

NORTH PORTLAND
Beaterville Cafe
Café Marx
El Burrito Loco
King Burrito
Magpie Cafe
Widmer Gasthaus

NORTHEAST, BEYOND 39TH
El Burrito Loco
McMenamin's Kennedy School
Pho Hung
Prescott Cafe

Taqueria El Vale
Yen Ha
Zien Hong

NORTHEAST, CLOSE IN
Albertina's
Bridges
Counter Culture
Doris' Cafe
Ensenada's
Horn of Africa

NORTHWEST
Acapulco's Gold
Besaw's
Big Dan's West Coast Bento
The Brazen Bean
BridgePort Brew Pub
Caffe Fresco
Dogs Dig
Elephants Delicatessen
Epicure
Escape From New York Pizza
Foothill Broiler
Garbonzos
The Gypsy
Jamie's
Justa Pasta Company
Kornblatt's Delicatessen
L'Auberge Bistro
La Buca
Marsee Baking
Mio Sushi
Misohapi
Noah's New York Bagels
Nob Hill Bar & Grill
Phil's Uptown Meat Market
Pizzicato
Portland Brewhouse Taproom and
  Grill
Stepping Stone
Swagat
Tara Thai Northwest
Thai Orchid
Typhoon!

OLD TOWN
Dan and Louis' Oyster Bar
Fellini
Shanghai Tunnel

PEARL DISTRICT
Bima Bar
Bridgeport Brew Pub
Cindy's Helvetia Cafe
Fuller's Coffee Shop
Holden's
Hoyt Street Cafe
Little Wing Cafe
Low Brow Lounge
Pearl Bakery

RIVERPLACE
Harborside Restaurant and
  Pilsner Room

SE DIVISION
Clay's Smokehouse Grill
Fusion
Los 3 Hermanos
Nature's Marketplace
Saigon Kitchen

SE POWELL
Campbell's Barbecue
Manila's Best
Pho Hung
Tennessee Red's
Thanh Thao

SELLWOOD
El Palenque
Gino's Restaurant and Bar

SOUTHEAST, BEYOND 39TH
Flying Pie Pizzeria
Mama's Corner Cafe
Pho Van
Sushi Takahashi
Taqueria Chavez
Thai Touch Cuisine

SOUTHEAST, CLOSE IN
Anne Hughes Kitchen Table Cafe
Caswell
J + M Cafe

Junior's Cafe
La Calaca Comelana
Le Bistro Montage
Monte Carlo Restaurant
Nicholas' Restaurant
Old Wives' Tales
Produce Row Cafe
Taco del Mar
Tenessee Red's
Zell's Cafe

ST. JOHNS
Czaba's Bar-B-Que and Catering
John Street Cafe
Super Burrito Express

SW MACADAM AVE-JOHNS
  LANDING
Bai Tong
Macheezmo Mouse
Noho's Hawaiian Cafe
Old Spaghetti Factory
Shanghai Noble House Restaurant
Stanich's West

WEST HILLS
Hands on Cafe
Ichiban
Nancy Lee's Pharmacy Fountain
Pizza Luna
Pizzicato
Skyline Restaurant
Vista Spring Cafe

WESTMORELAND
Bella Coola
Marsee Baking
Pizzicato
Saburo's
Stickers Asian Cafe

WOODSTOCK
Delta Cafe
Woodstock Wine and Deli

portland environs

BEAVERTON
Dingo's Taco Bar
Giovanni's Italian Restaurant
Ikenohana
Jamie's
Macheezmo Mouse
Marinepolis
McCormick and Schmick's
Nature's Marketplace
Noah's New York Bagels
Nonna Emilia Ristorante Italiano
Pho Hung
Siam Thai
Swagat

CLACKAMAS
Macheezmo Mouse

GRESHAM
Buster's Texas-Style Barbecue
El Burrito Loco
Pizzicato

HILLSBORO
Cornelius Pass Roadhouse and
   Brewery
Helvetia Tavern
Macheezmo Mouse

LAKE OSWEGO
Giant Drive-In
Gourmet Productions Market,
   Fine Food and Catering
Marsee Baking
Nature's Marketplace
Noah's New York Bagels
Thai Villa
Wu's Open Kitchen

MILWAUKIE
Buster's Texas-Style Barbecue
Super Burrito Express

OAK HILLS
Pizzicato
TK's Smokehouse and
   BBQ Company

PORTLAND AIRPORT
Macheezmo Mouse
Marsee Baking

RALEIGH HILLS
Hot Lips Pizza
Raccoon Lodge

TIGARD
Buster's Texas-Style Barbecue
Macheezmo Mouse
Wu's Open Kitchen

TUALATIN
Cocina del Sol

WEST LINN
Pizzicato
Thai Orchid

**VANCOUVER, WA AND
   VICINITY**
Buster's Texas-Style Barbecue
Dante's Ristorante
Holland Restaurant
Nature's Marketplace
Thai Little Home
Thai Orchid

food type index

AMERICAN
Alameda Brewhouse
Albertina's
Anne Hughes Kitchen Table Cafe
Besaw's
Caswell
Foothill Broiler
Fuller's Coffee Shop
The Gypsy
Harborside Restaurant and
    Pilsner Room
Holland Restaurant
Hoyt Street Cafe
Jake's Grill
John Street Cafe
Ken's Home Plate
Nancy Lee's Pharmacy Fountain
Old Spaghetti Factory
The Original Pancake House
Perry's on Fremont
Red Coach Restaurant
Zell's Cafe

BAGELS
Goldberg's Bakery
Kornblatt's Delicatessen
Marsee Baking
Noah's New York Bagels

BAKERIES
Elephants Delicatessen
Goldberg's Bakery
Grand Central Bakery and Cafe
Marsee Baking
Pazzoria Bakery and Cafe
Pearl Bakery

BARBECUE
Buster's Texas-Style Barbecue
Campbell's Barbeque
Clay's Smokehouse Grill
Czaba's Bar-B-Que and Catering
Tennessee Red's
TK's Smokehouse & BBQ Company

BENTO
Big Dan's West Coast Bento
Misohapi
Phil's Uptown Meat Market
Toney Bento

BISTROS
Bella Coola
Besaw's
Bravo Italia
Bread and Ink Cafe
Caswell
Chez What? Cafe
Counter Culture
Higgins Bar
L'Auberge Bistro
Marco's Cafe and Espresso Bar
Southpark Wine Bar

BREAKFAST
The Alameda Cafe
Beaterville Cafe
Besaw's
Bravo Italia
Bread and Ink Cafe
Bridges
Cadillac Cafe
Caffe Fresco
Cafe Lena
Café Marx
Chez What? Cafe
Cindy's Helvetia Cafe
The Cup and Saucer Cafe
Fat City Cafe
Fuller's Coffee Shop
The Gypsy
Hands on Cafe
Henry's Cafe
Holden's
Holland Restaurant
Hoyt Street Cafe
J + M Cafe
John Street Cafe

Junior's Cafe
Kornblatt's Delicatessen
Laurelthirst Public House
Lorn and Dottie's Luncheonette
Mama's Corner Cafe
Marco's Cafe and Espresso Bar
The Original Pancake House
Prescott Cafe
Red Electric Cafe
Stepping Stone
Suzanne's at Beaumont Village
Zell's Cafe

BREWPUBS
Alameda Brewhouse
BridgePort Brew Pub
Cornelius Pass Roadhouse
  and Brewery
Harborside Restaurant and
  Pilsner Room
McMenamin's Kennedy School
Portland Brewhouse Taproom
  and Grill
Raccoon Lodge
Rock Bottom Restaurant
  and Brewery
Widmer Gasthaus

BURGERS (see also BREWPUBS, DINERS, PUB GRUB)
Besaw's
BridgePort Ale House
Giant Drive-In
Foothill Broiler
Jamie's
L'Auberge Bistro
Perry's on Fremont
Red Coach Restaurant
Raccoon Lodge
Skyline Restaurant
Stanich's

CAFES (see also BREAKFAST, SOUP/SALAD/SANDWICH)
The Alameda Cafe
Beaterville Cafe
Bravo Italia
Cadillac Cafe
Cafe Lena
Caffe Fresco
Café Marx

The Cup and Saucer
Cup O' Cheer Cafe
The Empire Room
Grand Central Bakery and Cafe
Henry's Cafe
Holden's
Hoyt Street Cafe
John Street Cafe
Leaf and Bean Cafe
Magpie Cafe
Mama's Corner Cafe
Prescott Cafe
Pumpernickles
Red Electric Cafe
Suzanne's at Beaumont Village
Zell's Cafe

CAJUN/CREOLE
Delta Cafe
Le Bistro Montage

CARIBBEAN
Bima Bar
Salvador Molly's Sun Stop Cafe
Sweetwater's Jam House

CENTRAL AMERICAN
El Palenque
L'il Mexico Restaurant

CHINESE
Fong Chong
Formosa Harbor
Fujin
Good Day Restaurant
Shanghai Noble House Restaurant
Wu's Open Kitchen
Zien Hong

COFFEEHOUSES
Anne Hughes Kitchen Table Cafe
Cafe Lena
Common Grounds Coffeehouse
Henry's Cafe
Morning Star Espresso
Pearl Bakery
The Pied Cow
Pumpernickles

DELIS
Cup O' Cheer Cafe
Elephants Delicatessen

Goldberg's Bakery
Golden Loaf Bakery and Deli
Gourmet Productions Market,
   Fine Foods and Catering
Kornblatt's Delicatessen
Nature's Marketplace
Noah's New York Bagels
Woodstock Wine and Deli

DESSERTS/ICE CREAM
The Brazen Bean
Bravo Italia
The Empire Room
Grand Central Bakery and Cafe
Higgins Bar
L'Auberge Bistro
Southpark Wine Bar

DINERS
Cadillac Cafe
Cindy's Helvetia Cafe
Fat City Cafe
Fuller's Coffee Shop
Lorn and Dottie's Luncheonette
Nancy Lee's Pharmacy Fountain
Prescott Cafe
Red Coach Restaurant

ETHIOPIAN
Horn of Africa
Jarra's Ethiopian Restaurant

FILIPINO
Manila's Best

GUATEMALAN
L'il Mexico Restaurant

GERMAN
Widmer Gasthaus

GREEK
Nicholas' Restaurant

HAPPY HOUR
Chez's Lounge at Chez Grill
The Gypsy
Harborside Restaurant and
   Pilsner Room
Jake's Grill
McCormick and Schmick's
Stickers Asian Cafe

HAWAIIAN
Noho's Hawaiian Cafe

HOT DOGS/SAUSAGE
Good Dog/Bad Dog

INDIAN
India Oven
Swagat
The Tao of Tea

INTERNATIONAL
The Western Culinary Institute

INVENTIVE ETHNIC
Bella Coola
Caswell
Chez What? Cafe
Chez Jose East/Chez Jose West
Cocina del Sol
Counter Culture
Fellini
Fusion
Hands on Cafe
Ken's Home Plate
Macheezmo Mouse
Marco's Cafe and Espresso Bar
Old Wives' Tales

ITALIAN
Dante's Ristorante
Gino's Restaurant and Bar
Giovanni's Italian Restaurant
Justa Pasta Company
La Buca
Monte Carlo Restaurant
Nonna Emilia Ristorante Italiano
Old Spaghetti Factory
Pasta Bella
Pasta Veloce
Pazzoria Bakery and Cafe

JAPANESE
Big Dan's West Coast Bento
Ichiban
Ikenohana
Marinepolis
Mio Sushi
Saburo's
Sushi Takahashi
Toney Bento

KID FRIENDLY
Aztec Willie & Joey Rose Taqueria
Bangkok Kitchen
Chez Jose East/Chez Jose West
Cocina del Sol
Dan and Louis' Oyster Bar
Fat City Cafe
Flying Pie Pizzeria
Foothill Broiler
Garbonzos
Grand Central Bakery and Cafe
Giant Drive-In
Gino's Restaurant and Bar
Gourmet Productions Market, Fine
  Foods and Catering
Ichiban
Jamie's
Marco's Cafe and Espresso Bar
Macheezmo Mouse
Marinepolis
Old Spaghetti Factory
Old Wives' Tales
Perry's on Fremont
Salvador Molly's Sun Spot Cafe
Sushi Takahashi
Vista Spring Cafe
Wu's Open Kitchen

KOSHER
Noah's New York Bagels, Hillsdale

LAOTIAN
Tara Thai Northwest

LATE NIGHT
The Brazen Bean
Cassidy's
Dots Cafe
Fellini
Garbonzos
La Cruda
Laurelthirst Public House
Le Bistro Montage
Low Brow Lounge
Shanghai Tunnel
1201 Cafe and Lounge

LOUNGES
The Brazen Bean
Cassidy's
Dots Cafe

The Empire Room
Fellini
The Gypsy
Low Brow Lounge
Shanghai Tunnel
1201 Cafe and Lounge

MEXICAN
Acapulco's Gold
Aztec Willie & Joey Rose Taqueria
Cocina del Sol
Dingo's Taco Bar
El Burrito Loco
El Palenque
Ensenada's
King Burrito
La Calaca Comelona
La Cruda
La Sirenita
L'il Mexico Restaurant
Los 3 Hermanos
Macheezmo Mouse
Mi Ranchito Taqueria
Super Burrito Express
Taco Del Mar
Taqueria Chavez
Taqueria El Vale

MIDDLE EASTERN
Garbonzos
The Golden Loaf Bakery and Deli
Hoda's Middle Eastern Cuisine
Nicholas' Restaurant
Persian House Restaurant
Riyadh's

PAN-ASIAN
Misohapi
Stickers Asian Cafe

PIZZA (see also BREWPUBS, ITALIAN)
BridgePort Ale House
Escape from New York
Flying Pie Pizzeria
Hot Lips Pizza
Oasis Cafe
Pizza Luna
Pizzicato
Southpark Wine Bar
Vista Spring Cafe

PUB GRUB

Alameda Brewhouse
Bridgeport Ale House
BridgePort Brew Pub
Cassidy's
Cornelius Pass Roadhouse
  and Brewery
Goose Hollow Inn
The Gypsy
Harborside Restaurant
  and Pilsner Room
Helvetia Tavern
Laurelthirst Public House
McMenamin's Kennedy School
Nob Hill Bar & Grill
Portland Brewhouse Taproom
  and Grill
Produce Row
Raccoon Lodge
Rock Bottom Restaurant
  and Brewery
Stanich's
Widmer Gasthaus

SALVADORAN

El Palenque

SEAFOOD

Bima Bar
Dan and Louis' Oyster Bar
Dingo's Taco Bar

SOMALIAN

Horn of Africa

SOUP/SALAD/SANDWICH (see also BAKERIES, CAFES, DELIS, PUB GRUB)

Anne Hughes Kitchen Table Cafe
Bogart's
Bridges
Common Grounds Coffeehouse
Holden's
J + M Cafe
Leaf and Bean Cafe
Little Wing Cafe
Morning Star Espresso
Nature's Marketplace
Pazzoria Bakery and Cafe
Pumpernickles

SOUTHERN (see also BARBECUE, CAJUN/CREOLE)

Bima Bar
Delta Cafe
Doris' Cafe
Le Bistro Montage

SOUTHWESTERN

Chez Jose East/Chez Jose West
Chez's Lounge at Chez Grill
Salvador Molly's Sun Spot Cafe

TAKEOUT (see also ASIAN, DELIS, PIZZA)

Big Dan's West Coast Bento
Bravo Italia
Counter Culture
Dingo's Taco Bar
Dogs Dig
El Burrito Loco
El Palenque
Elephants Delicatessen
Epicure
Giant Drive-In
Gourmet Productions Market,
  Fine Foods and Catering
Holden's
Justa Pasta Company
Ken's Home Plate
Nature's Marketplace
Phil's Uptown Meat Market
Pumpernickles
Super Burrito Express
Suriya Thai
Thai Orchid
Thai Touch
Thanh Thao

TAPAS

Bella Coola
Colosso

TEAHOUSES

The Tao of Tea

THAI

Bai Tong
Bangkok Kitchen
Misohapi
Saigon Kitchen

Siam Thai
Suriya Thai
Talesi Thai Cuisine
Tara Thai Northwest
Thai Little Home
Thai Orchid
Thai Touch Cuisine
Thai Villa
Thanh Thao
Typhoon!

VEGETARIAN
Dogs Dig
Leaf and Bean Cafe
Marco's Cafe and Espresso Bar
Old Wives' Tales
The Tao of Tea

VIETNAMESE
Lanai Cafe
Pho Hung
Pho Van
Misohapi
Saigon Kitchen
Thanh Thao
Yen Ha
Zien Hong

WINE BARS
Bella Coola
The Empire Room
Southpark Wine Bar

portland cheap eats
report form

Based on my personal experience, I wish to nominate the following restaurant as a "Cheap Eat"; or confirm/correct/disagree with the current review.

_____
_____
_____
_____

(Please include address and telephone number of establishment, if convenient.)

Report:

Please describe food, service, style, comfort, value, date of visit, and other aspects of your experience; continue on other side if necessary.

_____
_____
_____
_____
_____
_____

I am not concerned, directly or indirectly, with the management or ownership of this establishment.

Signed _____
Address _____
_____
Phone _____
Date _____

Please address to *Portland Cheap Eats* and send to:

Sasquatch Books
615 Second Avenue, Suite 260
Seattle, WA 98104

Feel free to email feedback as well: books@SasquatchBooks.com

portland **cheap eats**
report form

Based on my personal experience, I wish to nominate the following restaurant as a "Cheap Eat"; or confirm/correct/disagree with the current review.

_____

_____

_____

_____

(Please include address and telephone number of establishment, if convenient.)

Report:

Please describe food, service, style, comfort, value, date of visit, and other aspects of your experience; continue on other side if necessary.

_____

_____

_____

_____

_____

_____

I am not concerned, directly or indirectly, with the management or ownership of this establishment.

Signed _____

Address _____

_____

Phone _____

Date _____

Please address to *Portland Cheap Eats* and send to:

Sasquatch Books
615 Second Avenue, Suite 260
Seattle, WA 98104

Feel free to email feedback as well: books@SasquatchBooks.com